"He delivered us
from the domain of darkness,
and transferred us
to the kingdom of His beloved Son."
—*Apostle Paul, Colossians 1:13*

About the Editors

James R. Adair began his career as a reporter for *The Asheville (N.C.) Citizen* and joined the editorial staff of Scripture Press Publications, Inc., in 1945. He served as editor of the firm's *Power*/Line Papers until the mid-'70s, when he became involved full time in the Victor Books Division of Scripture Press. He currently serves as Executive Editor of Victor Books. He has written a number of books, including *The Man from Steamtown* (Moody Press), *M.R. DeHaan: the Man and His Ministry* (Zondervan), and *Surgeon on Safari* (for Dr. Paul Jorden) (Hawthorn). Books he has compiled and edited include *God's Power Within* and *God's Power to Triumph* (both Prentice-Hall). Mr. Adair lives in Wheaton, Illinois, is married (Virginia), and is father of two daughters (Mary and Martha). He is a member of Wheaton Bible Church.

Ted Miller joined the editorial staff of Scripture Press Publications, Inc. in 1951 after earning his M.A. in journalism from Northwestern University. He served as associate editor of *Power,* the forerunner of *Power for Living.* He joined the editorial staff of Tyndale House, Wheaton in 1964 to edit *The Christian Reader,* which he originated. Mr. Miller has edited or written a number of books. He compiled *He Touched Me* (Harvest), is coauthor of *Whatever Happened to Eden?* (Tyndale) and wrote *Say It with Love* for Dr. Howard Hendricks, a book that Billy Graham selected for TV distribution. Mr. Miller also lives in Wheaton, attends Wheaton Bible Church, is married (Jeanne), and is father of four sons (Jim, Rich, Jon, and Bob).

ESCAPE FROM DARKNESS

compiled by

JAMES R. ADAIR and TED MILLER

This book is designed for both individual reading and group study. A Leader's Guide with Victor Multiuse Transparency Masters is available from your local bookstore or from the publisher.

VICTOR BOOKS
a division of SP Publications, Inc.
WHEATON, ILLINOIS 60187

Offices also in Fullerton, California • Whitby, Ontario, Canada • Amersham-on-the-Hill, Bucks, England

Unless otherwise noted, Scripture quotations are from the *New American Standard Bible* (NASB), © 1960, 1962, 1971, 1972, 1973 by The Lockman Foundation, La Habra, California. Other quotations are from the *King James Version* (KJV); *The Living Bible* (LB), © 1971, Tyndale House Publishers, Wheaton, Illinois; *Good News Bible (Today's English Version,* TEV), © 1976, American Bible Society, New York; and *New International Version* (NIV), © 1978 by The New York International Bible Society. Used by permission.

Recommended Dewey Decimal Classification: 291.42
   Suggested Subject Heading: COMPARATIVE RELIGION; RELIGIOUS EXPERIENCE

Library of Congress Catalog Card Number: 82-50329
ISBN: 0-88207-318-4

© 1982 by SP Publications, Inc. All rights reserved
Printed in the United States of America

VICTOR BOOKS
A division of SP Publications, Inc.
P.O. Box 1825 • Wheaton, Illinois 60187

Contents

"What Is Truth?" / Preface 7
1 I Was Captured by the Children of God / Pennee Joh 9
2 The Wierwille Way Trapped Me / Connie M. Heidebrecht 22
3 I Was a False Witness / William Cetnar 31
4 In and Out of Mormonism / Marolyn Wragg 38
5 Why I Left Christian Science / Carolyn Poole 46
6 I Eluded Armstrong's Clutch / Joe Mehesy 54
7 I Was an Agnostic Unitarian / Elizabeth Kanouse 60
8 Unity Almost Splintered My Faith / Faye Myers 66
9 I Talked with Spirits / Victor Ernest 71
10 The Moonies Almost Got Me / Anonymous 80
11 Maharishi, Meditation, and Me / Reuben B. Rubin 86
12 Hare Krishna Starved My Soul / Ed Senesi 92
13 Allah Failed to Answer Me / Anonymous 101
14 I Worshiped a Million Gods / Rita Sairsingh 109
15 Zen Buddhism Blinded Me / Lit-sen Chang 114
16 My Life as an Atheist / William J. Murray 122
17 Satan Shackled My Soul / Marie Moore 129
18 Hedonism Put Me behind Bars / Gwynn Lewis 134
19 Clues to the Cults / Dave Breese 143
20 God's Way / Billy Graham / Epilogue 151

The authors and publisher gratefully acknowledge permission to reprint the following:

"I Was Captured by the Children of God," *The Trim Tab*, publication for the Fellowship of Christian Airline Personnel, Fayetteville, Ga.; © 1981 by Pennee Joh.

"The Wierwille Way Trapped Me," © 1982 by Connie M. Heidebrecht.

"I Was a False Witness," *Eternity*, © 1980 by Evangelical Ministries, Inc., Philadelphia, Pa.

"In and Out of Mormonism," permission of BIOLA University.

"Why I Left Christian Science," © 1981 by Carolyn Poole, Lancaster, Calif.

"I Eluded Armstrong's Clutch," © 1980 by *Evangel*, Winona Lake, Ind.

"I Was an Agnostic Unitarian," *The Presbyterian Journal*, Asheville, N.C., © 1980 by Elizabeth Kanouse.

"Unity Almost Splintered My Faith," *Insight*, Grand Rapids, Mich., © 1981 by Faye Myers.

"I Talked with Spirits," excerpted from the book by the same title, © 1970, Tyndale House Publishers, Inc., Wheaton, Ill.

"The Moonies Almost Got Me," © 1978 by *The Church Herald*, Grand Rapids, Mich.

"Maharishi, Meditation, and Me," *Power for Living*, © 1977 by Scripture Press Publications, Inc., Wheaton, Ill.

"Hare Krishna Starved My Soul," *Cornerstone*, © 1981, Jesus People U.S.A, Chicago.

"Allah Failed to Answer Me," excerpted from the book *The True Path* by Mark Hannah, © 1975 International Students, Colorado Springs, Colo.

"I Worshiped a Million Gods," © 1972 by *Church of God Evangel*, Cleveland, Tenn.

"Zen Buddhism Blinded Me," excerpted from the book *Zen Existentialism* by Lit-sen Chang, © 1969, Presbyterian and Reformed Publishing Co., Phillipsburg, N.J.

"Satan Shackled My Soul," *FreeWay*, © 1978 by Scripture Press Publications, Inc., Wheaton, Ill.

"Hedonism Put Me Behind Bars," © 1977 by *Campus Life*, Wheaton, Ill.

"Clues to the Cults," excerpted from the book *Know the Marks of Cults* by Dave Breese, © 1980 by Scripture Press Publications, Inc. and published by Victor Books, Wheaton, Ill.

"God's Way," *Decision*, © 1963 by The Billy Graham Evangelistic Association, Minneapolis, Minn.

Preface

"What Is Truth?"

"Thou hast made us for Thyself and the heart of man is restless until it finds its rest in Thee," declared Augustine, the fourth-century Christian theologian. Across the ancient East and the younger West, men and women, young and old, search for spiritual reality. The quest is perilous and confusing, as these true stories show. For, as Solomon said, "God made men upright, but they have sought out many devices" (Ecclesiastes 7:29).

"What is truth?" asked the Roman governor, Pilate, to Jesus of Nazareth. Jesus' answer by His whole life was: "I am the way, the truth, and the life" (John 14:6). Some of the authors of these contemporary stories almost lost their lives before finding new life in Jesus Christ. Others experienced profound darkness before sighting the light of the world in Jesus. All now rest from their anxious pursuit of the true way to God.

It is fascinating and frightening to see how ingeniously the world's prophets, messiahs, and gods contradict each other and claim exclusive truth for themselves. But despite the parade of world religions and their offshoot cults, sincere seekers will find the truth and be set free, according to the promise of Jesus confirmed by these modern pilgrims who journeyed from "darkness to light."

James R. Adair / Ted Miller

SECTION 1
The Cult Trip

1
I Was Captured by the Children of God

*by Pennee Joh
as told to Sammye Vieh*

I was privileged to grow up in a close family, the youngest of five children. We moved to Atlanta from Florida when I was 13, and I attended church regularly with my family until I graduated from high school in 1971. At 18, I moved out of my parents' house and got a job as a secretary at Georgia Tech.

In 1972 I went to a Billy Graham crusade in Atlanta, and for the first time in my life I heard the Gospel with my heart and not just my ears. I eagerly walked to the front of the gathering and prayed to receive Christ into my life.

Pennee Joh is an airline stewardess who lives in Union City, Georgia.
Sammye Vieh is editor of *The Trim Tab,* publication for the Fellowship of Christian Airline Personnel, Fayetteville, Georgia.

The following year a major airline hired me as a flight attendant, but after training I was immediately laid off. While waiting for a job opening, I worked for an investment firm. Then romance clashed with my young faith.

The young man I had been dating for three years began discussing marriage. I wanted to marry him, but he was not a Christian, and I wanted a spiritual foundation in my marriage. During this time of indecision I started thinking about God's will and I desired to know what the Bible teaches.

Also, I was reading Hal Lindsey's *The Late Great Planet Earth*, which caused me to reflect on my Christian position. I had always believed in God, but I had never learned that the Bible is God's guidebook for daily living. My Bible knowledge was pretty much limited to the Ten Commandments and the birth and crucifixion of Jesus.

Early in 1976 I moved into a condominium with my 24-year-old brother, Fritz, an engineering graduate from Georgia Tech. A dedicated Christian, Fritz was excited to see my interest in spiritual growth. Yet we spent little time sharing our concerns because both of us now had traveling jobs and seldom touched home base at the same time.

As the days went by, I began to hunger for spiritual resources. I would talk about the Lord to anybody who would talk with me. I wanted to share what I knew and also to learn from other Christians. I didn't try to find a church because I thought they were all alike, and I hadn't learned much from the ones in my past. I kept searching and studying on my own, and the more I learned, the more I realized that I had grieved a holy God. I yearned to grow in knowledge, but with no church, teaching, or Christian fellowship, I only struggled in that direction.

Looking back now, I realize I was too gullible, sensitive, and trusting toward people. Though I had been on my own for several years, I was still protected by my family and not wise in the ways of the world.

On February 6, 1976 I had a flight layover in New York City. That night I had a dream that drastically affected my life. Christians were being raptured to heaven, but the angels didn't look like I expected. They were unkempt with long, stringy, dirty hair. They tried to yank me up to heaven and called me unkind names in mean voices.

I Was Captured by the Children of God / 11

As they hovered over me, I said, "I thought the Rapture was supposed to be beautiful, with music and trumpets."

They yelled, "Do you want to go to heaven or don't you?"

I started crying and said, "Yes," so they pulled me up to heaven—which looked like an earth covered with litter and pollution.

Then I met "God." He was short, fat, and had gray, thin hair. I quickly got over my disappointment because he was gentle and loving. He put his hands in a pot of black, molten wax, formed a calf which came to life, and gave it to me. That impressed me, but I couldn't see any of my family there and I asked how I could get my family to heaven. He told me to live for God 100 percent, and gave me coins to use a pay phone to call back to earth. Just then my alarm clock rang and I woke up, but the dream was not easy to shake off.

The vividness of my dream stayed with me all day, and I felt strangely rejuvenated by it. I was so excited that I told the other girls on my trip about it.

When I got home, the phone was ringing. It was a girlfriend calling to invite me over. When I arrived I saw that quite a few of our mutual friends were present, and I wanted so much to discuss Christ with them. When I tried, they said, "P.J., this isn't the time or the place. Come on, get off the subject!" There were some Jewish friends visiting, so I started talking to them about Judaism because Jesus was a Jew and I wanted to know about that faith. I tried to explain the Gospel to them, but they threw questions at me I couldn't understand. In a feeble way, I described my faith to them, then I left.

From there I drove to a Baskin Robbins in the Buckhead area to get ice cream for a friend's birthday party the next day. It was already dark, and I wanted to deliver it to his apartment at Georgia Tech before heading home. As I left the ice cream parlor, I was confronted by a young man and woman, unkempt in appearance. Our conversation went:

"May we talk with you?"

"Yes, of course."

"Are you a Christian?"

"Yes! Are you?"

"We are Christian missionaries."

"Do you read the Bible?"

12 / Escape from Darkness

They handed me one. It was a *King James Version* and looked as if it had seen much use.

"We have forsaken all and are living as the first Christians did in the Book of Acts," one said.

I was vaguely familiar with the Book of Acts, but didn't remember reading any of it. To meet and talk with these people seemed like a small miracle! My mind went back to the dream I'd had the previous night. In it, "God" had told me to live for him 100 percent, and these people were saying the same thing! Their names were Pilgrim and Mary Magdalene, they said.

By this time it was 9 P.M. and the temperature was about 30 degrees. When Pilgrim asked if I would like to talk more at the church, I said yes. They had no transportation, so I offered them a ride, explaining that first I had to deliver the ice cream to my friend's apartment. When we arrived there, I walked in and out without stopping to talk. Pilgrim and Magdalene were more important to me.

They directed me to their "church," which was actually an old house in a downtown district of Atlanta. As I met the other members, I was deeply impressed by their love. They all had big smiles and welcomed me with hugs. As they began to explain their beliefs, I decided it was a strongly Bible-structured group.

To them, I was plainly a "babe," a "sheep" in the perspective of God. Conversations were punctuated with an ongoing chant: "Praise the Lord . . . hallelujah . . . thank You, Jesus."

It was 3 A.M. when I finally got a chance to sleep. I had a cot in a room with two other women. As I lay there gazing at a street-light shining through the window, I wondered if I was where God wanted me to be. Soon I drifted off to sleep.

I was awakened three hours later, at 6 o'clock. Since it was Sunday, considered a day of rest, there was no legwork on the streets—just household chores. I was glad to help any way I could—clean the kitchen, bathroom, or whatever. Women and children scurried around in all directions.

After a rather skimpy breakfast, a man named Samson and his wife began talking with me. They played some taped testimonies of people who had joined them—"the Children of God," they called themselves. The testimonies sounded impressive, but I had little opportunity to say anything in return. I felt bad when they told me some airline pilots in Boston had donated money to their cause but were too wrapped up in worldly things to forsake all—they called them "systemites."

When Samson and his wife slowed down, Pilgrim and Magdalene came in and took up the indoctrination. Occasionally others came into the room and asked how Pilgrim had found this "little sheepy."

We all gathered in a circle to sing and chant praises, and after a time Samson and Pilgrim interrupted it to announce that the Lord had directed them to change my name to Rebekah. I was like Rebekah in the story of Abraham and Isaac, they said.

Before the evening was over, I signed a paper giving the Children of God power of attorney over my possessions, though I did not understand what I was doing.

When Pilgrim and Mary Magdalene mentioned they had to do their laundry, I invited them to use the washing machine and dryer at my condominium. They accepted, and we went together.

The wash took a long time, and because it was late, I suggested that Pilgrim and Magdalene stay with me overnight. They agreed, but before we retired the phone rang. It was the girlfriend who had invited me over the day before—a lifetime ago! She said her grandfather had died and she asked to spend the night at my place because I lived near the airport, and she had an early morning flight to catch.

Instead of answering her question, I told her I was going to be a Christian missionary and planned to quit my job with the airline. She pleaded, "Don't quit, P.J.; take a leave of absence!" I countered with the advice that she was living in sin and should seek the Lord with all her heart. In the background, Pilgrim and Magdalene urged me to hang up, warning that my friends and family were of the devil's world and would try to talk me out of God's calling. Convinced, I hung up the phone.

Unknown to me, my girlfriend immediately called a mutual friend and repeated our conversation. Frightened, the listener said I had been brainwashed or hypnotized and suggested that my parents be notified.

While the phone lines were buzzing, Pilgrim and Magdalene retired to their sleeping bags on the living room floor and I to my room upstairs. Suddenly I heard the front door open, and I went back downstairs. It was my brother, Fritz, home after a long drive from Florida. He was reading a note I had left explaining my plans. I had signed it "Rebekah," my new name. Grinning happily, I said, "You know how long I've been looking, Fritz; well, I've found it! These are my new friends, Pilgrim and Mary Magdalene."

He stared at me, speechless. The silence was broken by the phone. Fritz answered, and I heard one side of the conversation. Fritz said he had driven almost all night from Florida, and he didn't know what was going on. He would "sleep on it" and call in the morning. Then he gave the phone to me. My agitated mother was seeking information, and I assured her that I was all right, and had decided to be a missionary. We couldn't communicate very well at that hour of the night, so soon said good night.

At 8 the next morning, my mother, father, and uncle, who is an ordained minister, walked into my bedroom. Magdalene and I were sitting on my bed reading the Bible, and Pilgrim was shaving in Fritz's bathroom. My brother had already left for work after calling my parents.

"Pennee, aren't you going to fix breakfast?" Mother asked.

"I'm having my food," I said, and pointed to the Bible.

But my family insisted we go downstairs and talk. Before Pilgrim, Magdalene, and I followed them downstairs, Pilgrim prayed that Satan would be bound, and that my parents wouldn't persuade me to leave the mission field.

First, my mother asked me what I was doing. I said I was giving my life to Christ and would be serving Him fulltime. Other questions followed, and I looked to Pilgrim again and again for answers which he obligingly gave. Exasperated, my parents demanded that I speak for myself, but I could only look again at Pilgrim for assistance.

Finally, my mother suggested that I go home with them, build a nice fire in the fireplace, and share my thoughts and plans. Pilgrim stated emphatically that this would be impossible. Then a big argument erupted, ending in my father phoning the police to expel the visitors.

The police arrived and listened to our story. On learning that I was 22 years old, the policeman told Mom and Dad I could not be prevented from making my own decisions. But he added, "Young lady, not many parents care about their children as yours have demonstrated they do; I think you should go with them." I looked at Pilgrim and again he said no.

I Was Captured by the Children of God / 15

We three left to get my car, and Daddy grabbed me by the arm. "Pennee, you're not going with them!" he shouted. The police stopped him, repeating that I was of age and could go wherever I wanted—it would be illegal for him to force me to do otherwise.

Pilgrim, Magdalene, and I went merrily on our way, chanting and praying as we left. They reinforced the point that my family was of Satan and that they would do anything to divert me from God's calling. They shared some stories about other missionaries with families who were demon possessed, and these parents had tried to kidnap the missionaries. I should beware of that possibility, they warned.

Scripture memorizing began for me that morning. I was to learn four Scriptures a day. As we rode along, they gave me my assignment for that day.

I admired Pilgrim—he had been with Children of God for six years, and was a relative of Moses David, the COG founder. He knew the Bible well and seemed to have deep faith.

At lunchtime, we drove to Grady Hospital. The group tries to eat cheaply, and the hospital food was low priced. Other days we went to restaurants where Pilgrim announced we were Christian missionaries and would appreciate free meals. Usually we received them.

After lunch, my new friends took me to a phone booth to call my supervisor at the airline where I worked to tell him I was quitting. "Aren't you going to give two weeks' notice?" he asked in surprise.

"No," I replied.

"Are you getting married?" he asked.

"Kind of," I answered. COG had told me I was now part of the "bride of Christ." My supervisor could only say OK.

We spent the rest of the day and all night in the apartment of a young Jewess whom Pilgrim was trying to recruit. He spent hours telling her about the COG, and I did my part, explaining how the Lord had paved the road for me to devote my life to His service.

Early the next morning Pilgrim contacted the COG church, and they told him my brother had been there looking for me. Fritz expressed interest in joining COG and said he wanted to talk with me about it first. The church encouraged him to call again and said they would arrange a meeting with me.

After the call, Pilgrim drove to a shopping center for us to have our Bible study, then to "litness" among the shoppers. When we began selling our literature, however, a security guard demanded that we leave. "Systemite! The wrath of God is upon them," Pilgrim muttered. "I know a better place to litness."

He drove us to a major industrial boulevard in the city where we parked near a traffic light and got out. We stood on the concrete median and approached stopped cars when the light turned red. "We are Christian missionaries," we explained. "Will you help our cause with some change?" then we handed out a "Mo letter" written by Moses David (Brandt Berg). I wasn't very enthusiastic talking about him; I really wanted to share Jesus' love with people. Many responded, "I go to church." When I reported that to Pilgrim, he spat. "Systemites! Tell them that we are the church of Christ and God's new creation."

On one of Pilgrim's many phone checks with the church, he was told my brother had returned with a friend and wanted to see me. So we went back to the colony. Fritz talked with me alone, and he begged me to go home with him. He said I was being deceived, and that God didn't intend all His people to live together. I nervously flipped through my Bible, praying that God would show me some Scripture that supported my decision to be a missionary. Fritz tried in vain to convince me to leave.

While we were talking, the colony members recognized the friend who came with Fritz—he had helped remove another girl from COG three months earlier. The two were ordered off the property, so they left with Fritz vowing he would be back.

I learned later that when he got home where my family and friends were waiting, he told them: "She's really gone off the deep end! Somehow, we've got to get her away from that bunch of weirdos!"

The next morning, Wednesday, after the usual limited amount of sleep and food, we had our Bible study, Scripture memorizing, and a question-answer period. Anyone with a question wrote it down and put the paper in a box. Leaders emptied the box and gave their answers at the morning session.

After our lesson, the colony packed my VW with all sorts of stuff. Not till later did I learn we were headed for Mississippi to open a new colony. And following the conventional practice, I probably was to be married off to someone. No official weddings take place—men and women sleep together if they're interested, are "married" by the leader of the colony, and can be "divorced" anytime.

Before we left the church, someone looked outside to make sure we weren't being observed. Then Pilgrim went out, looked up and down the street, and motioned for me and Magdalene to get into the car.

Little did I know that my father, brother, sister, brother-in-law, and a neighbor were watching from down the street, just out of sight. They had spent the previous day planning my kidnaping. My father, a highly decorated Air Force pilot during World War II, planned and coordinated the details.

As we drove away from the church, my father's car fell in behind. He later said he ran stop signs and red lights, made illegal turns, and broke other traffic laws trying to keep up with us in the heavy traffic.

Many miles later, Pilgrim pulled into a school parking lot near a busy, four-lane highway. He and I were to go over my memorization while Magdalene went to the street corner to "litness."

The next thing I knew, Fritz had his arms wrapped around me tightly and was saying, "Penn, you're going to be OK; nobody's going to hurt you." Pilgrim started to grab me, but Fritz held me with one arm and cocked his other fist at Pilgrim, warning, "Don't you dare try to stop me!"

While I was pushed into my dad's car between my sister and Fritz, my brother-in-law was pulling a squealing Magdalene from my car and my dad was being restrained by his neighbor from slugging Pilgrim. My brother-in-law drove Dad's car, and Dad and the neighbor followed in mine. I twisted around and saw Pilgrim and Magdalene shaking their fists and screaming at the getaway cars.

My family took me straight to the home of people whose daughter had also been in COG. They were very friendly and invited me in for coffee or tea. At first, I refused to get out of the car. I said coffee and tea were impure, so I couldn't drink them. And I insisted they call me Rebekah.

Finally I was persuaded to go in the house. I sat down on the floor and refused to eat or drink anything. Later, I was told I tried to "share my testimony," but was incoherent and trembling pitifully.

My mother, after learning of my condition, got in touch with a psychiatrist who was acquainted with the aftereffects of cult programming. He agreed to see me immediately.

I was admitted to a hospital, where I remained for two and a half weeks. On the advice of the doctor and a lawyer, my father was made my legal guardian for 90 days. Pilgrim swore out a warrant for the arrest of my father for kidnaping me and stealing his possessions. When the police came to serve the warrant, my mother explained the situation, including the fact that I was under a doctor's care, and they dropped the matter. But my parents knew Pilgrim might still try to get me back, and legal guardianship gave them the right to protect me and my possessions from the COG.

The day after the rescue, while going through the "stuff" packed in my car, it became obvious why Pilgrim wanted his possessions returned. The "stuff" included incriminating evidence about the COG. There were lists of people's real names, their biblical names, their present locations, and their parents' names. There were Mo letters, hate-filled tirades against America, the church, and a variety of other institutions. My father turned these things over to the deputy attorney general.

I was miserable in the hospital. I was told not to talk about God or Jesus, and someone took my Bible away. I saw my doctor briefly once a day. Most of the staff had no conception of real Christianity, and all of their "help" was based on Freudian theories. Their predominant methods of treatment were drugs, yoga, and meditation. I would call my parents on the phone and beg them to take me home. I thought I would go crazy if they didn't get me out of there! I even agreed to talk to a deprogrammer.

My parents didn't know what to do, but they could see I wasn't getting any better in the hospital. They took me home, and my mother had to sleep with me because I was consumed with fear. I had been taught that the devil would attack anyone who left the calling of God, and I thought I was going to die.

My desperate parents called a deprogrammer who was working in another state with a Moonie recruit and arranged a meeting three days after I left the hospital.

My deprogrammer was a Christian who had been in COG for five years before coming out. In the presence of my brother Fritz, and a friend who had also been in COG, the deprogrammer began by establishing that COG was a cult and then explained how they brainwashed people. The hours marched on as I slowly absorbed facts and dissected information. No physical force was used and no threats were made.

As my deprogrammer explained it, cult leaders built up a wall in my mind, closing out my past and putting new thoughts into my head. Deprogramming would shoot holes in that wall by getting me to think straight again. In COG and other cults you're not allowed to think—they think for you. When you finally realize that you were conned, you usually react by fainting, crying, or laughing. It's at this point of emotional release that you are considered deprogrammed. When I finally understood, I laughed—hysterically. So did everybody else. I couldn't believe I had been so naive.

That was just the beginning, however. There were weeks of rehabilitation where I was deliberately put into decision-making situations, since cult victims usually lose ability to do this. Then there were months of finding my way back to a normal lifestyle. It usually takes a minimum of one year to get over the effects of cultic mind control.

There were many ups and downs over the next couple of years. I started flying again, strayed away from the Lord, and a year later was in an automobile accident requiring extensive medical care and another leave of absence from work. During this time, however, I continued to hear the gentle appeal of my Lord: "My sheep hear My voice" (John 10:27).

In 1980, I attended a convention of the Fellowship of Christian Airline Personnel, and that was a turning point in my life.

God has been, and continues to be, gracious to me. He protected me in the midst of religious wolves, brought me out of a dark valley, and placed my steps on the narrow road of life. Now I follow Jesus as Saviour and Lord of my life, and I grow daily in knowledge of Him and in love for Him.

Darkness vs. Light

The Children of God Say:

"If there is a choice between reading your Bible, I want to tell you that you had better read what God said today, in preference to what he said 2,000 years ago. Then when you've gotten done reading the latest MO letters, you can go back to reading the Bible." (Moses David, "Old Bottles," *MO Letter,* August 1973)

"When I get drunk, I yield to God's spirit. . . . If you get intoxicated, why, it just makes you even more free in the spirit—at least it does for me." (Moses David, "Jesus and Sex," *MO Letter,* March 1974)

"You must obey: implicitly, quickly, and without question your officers in the Lord, if you wish to remain a member of this team." (COG *Revolutionary Contract* for new members)

"We agree with 95% of the radical revolutionaries' goals, but their goal of utopia, they cannot reach, while we have reached it already. . . . We are practicing the only pure form of communism." (David Moses, "The Rise of the Reactionary Right," *MO Letter*)

The Bible Says:

"Heaven and earth will pass away, but My words will not pass away." (Jesus, *Mark* 13:31). "You shall not add to the word which I am commanding you, nor take away from it." (Moses, *Deuteronomy* 4:2)

"Do not get drunk with wine, for that is dissipation, but be filled with the Spirit." / "Drunkards . . . shall [not] inherit the kingdom of God." (Apostle Paul, *Ephesians* 5:18; *1 Corinthians* 6:10)

"Do not be called leaders; for one is your Leader, that is, Christ. But the greatest among you shall be your servant." (Jesus, *Matthew* 23:10-11)

"Let every person be in subjection to the governing authorities. . . . He who resists authority has opposed the ordinance of God." (Apostle Paul, *Romans* 13:1-2)

"God breaks up marriages in order that he might join each of the parties together with himself. He rips off wives, husbands, or children to make up his bride if the rest of the family refuses to follow.... If you have not forsaken your husband or wife for the Lord at some time or another, you have not forsaken all." (Moses David, "One Wife," *MO Letter*)

"God made them male and female. For this cause a man shall leave his father and mother, and the two shall become one flesh; consequently, they are no longer two, but one flesh. What therefore God has joined together, let no man separate." (Jesus, *Mark* 10:6-9)

"You, our parents, are the most God-defying, commandment-breaking, insanely rebellious rebels of all time, who are on the brink of destroying and polluting all of us and our world if we do not rise up against you in the name of God.... God is going to destroy you and save us." (Moses David, "Who Are The Rebels?" *MO Letter,* March 1970)

"There are many rebellious men, empty talkers and deceivers ... they are upsetting whole families, teaching things they should not teach, for the sake of sordid gain." (Apostle Paul, *Titus* 1:10-11)

2
The Wierwille Way Trapped Me

by Connie M. Heidebrecht

It was on August 4, 1979 that I checked into an Indianapolis motel with a determination which I had never before felt. I rented the room for two days, specifying that there be no maid service. My plan must not be interrupted because of a forgotten detail, and total seclusion was an intrinsic part of it. I had thought a great deal about this step. At first, the idea to end my life seemed as ludicrous as it was repugnant, but pressed by circumstances in my life, I believed suicide was the only solution.

Finally, ensconced in my room, with only my thoughts and memories as final companions, I swallowed a bottle of Darvon, a pain reliever, with half a fifth of whiskey and lay down on the motel bed to await death. As I lay there, thoughts of the past years bombarded my mind.

Soon after graduating high school in Wichita, Kansas, I had been excited to discover Victor Paul Wierwille and The Way. A friend whom I admired convinced me that The Way offered me and other young people the answers to all of life's problems. As the song inquires, "Who could ask for anything more?"

The author of this chapter, as the account indicates, resides in Wichita, Kansas and is currently enrolled in a Bible school.

The Wierwille Way Trapped Me / 23

We teens of the late '60s and early '70s were on a high-demand quest for personal fulfillment and peaceful reality; we were finding our identity and opening new vistas for mankind. Hallucinogens helped us reach our goal of self-actualization. We were, in many cases, throwing out Victorian values, and at the same time, wanting real answers and absolutes that would not change with each new social fad. Then into my life, and the lives of others like myself, swept the easy answers of The Way, International. With love and affirmation from a cadre of united young people, they extricated me from the tremendous pressure of having to make my own decisions—and eased me into a state of total dependency which lasted eight years and almost stole my life.

The Way is headquartered on a 147-acre farm just outside New Knoxville, Ohio southwest of Lima. Though there is no official membership, fellowships are active in all 50 states and 37 foreign countries. A defunct church college in Kansas purchased in 1974 was renamed The Way College of Emporia. It offers one- and two-year nonaccredited courses in biblical studies and houses members of The Way Corps, a four-year program to train leaders. The Way also owns The Way College of Biblical Research and Teaching in Rome City, Indiana. This facility was formerly a Roman Catholic convent and health resort with natural hot springs. Here live The Family Corps, which consists primarily of Way Corps older adult members and those with children.

The Way also owns Camp Gunnison in Gunnison, Colorado and has easy access to Total Fitness Institute, a wilderness retreat in southern California. This is run by Dr. John Somerville, a son-in-law of President-Founder Wierwille. Looking at its property, one might say The Way is solidly established.

The Way's charismatic leader and "Father-in-the-Word," "Doctor" Victor Paul Wierwille is a handsome, macho man in his mid-60s who manages to keep a tan the year round. A former minister in the Evangelical and Reformed Church (now the United Church of Christ), he claims to have heard God say, "I will teach you the Word as it has not been known since the first century, if you will only teach it." His movement started slowly and burst into national prominence with the explosion of the Jesus movement.

I found Dr. Wierwille a compelling speaker, with ability to easily influence crowds. Yet, he is a volatile personality, and he can change from congeniality to anger in an instant. In a class setting I have seen him suddenly go into a rage in speaking of ministers who he believed were critical of him or The Way. It is impossible to predict what his mood will be from moment to moment.

Wierwille demanded blind obedience from us and tolerated no dissension. Conversely, he demonstrated one of the most caring attitudes I have ever seen. When he said: "You're my people. God bless. I love you. You're the best," it was a rare person who did not respond positively. I did.

The power of The Way flows through its organization from the "root" to the distant "leaves," as in the life of a tree. The roots are planted firmly at international headquarters. The next level is the "trunk," the different countries where The Way is well established. Next are the "regions" (not exactly a botanical term, but another direct link was needed to insure control from the root). Then come the "limbs" which are individual state groups. From them issue the "branches," which are cities or areas containing several "twigs"—the individual in-home fellowships frequented by an average of 8 to 12 persons, who are the "leaves."

As spiritual nourishment from New Knoxville flows to the leaves, so financial sustenance pours back to New Knoxville. Thousands faithfully give in excess of 20 percent of their regular earnings to The Way. In addition, the major indoctrination tools, Power for Abundant Living (PFAL) class and literature, bring in a handsome profit to headquarters.

People are first attracted to The Way by the love and acceptance of twig members, but there would be no continuity and uniformity ("like-mindedness," The Way calls it) without the 36-hour PFAL class. It is offered on video tape, audio tape, and 16mm film. The enrollment card lists 10 PFAL claims and comes complete with a money-back guarantee if not satisfied. The impressive claims include teaching how to develop harmony in the home, discern truth from error, establish and maintain health, pray effectually, and develop financial prosperity. When I saw the green card, I was impressed! Who wouldn't be? It also claims to answer 95 percent of the most frequently asked questions about the Bible or life. All was offered for just $45 then—now at least $100. After I completed PFAL, I no longer could think thoughts that contradicted teachings of The Way.

PFAL was only the start however. I became involved in a

smorgasbord of seminars, classes, advanced study series, and fellowships five or six nights a week. How I managed to complete 51½ hours as a freshman at Friends University, I don't know. I do know that when I occasionally needed to miss an evening fellowship in order to study, a leader would question my priorities. Wasn't the goal (Word Over the World) important to me? Wasn't I able to trust God to give me the grades I needed?

Despite these danger signals, I delved more deeply into the teachings of The Way. At the end of my freshman year, I left not only home, family, and friends, but also my college, and with it my positions on the school newspaper and as a professor's assistant. My destination: New Knoxville, where I would take the Advanced Class on PFAL, and be commissioned as a Word Over the World (WOW) Ambassador.

The WOW Ambassador program is a one-year commitment to go anywhere in the U.S. (now foreign countries are included) to open new areas of outreach. Ambassadors devote 48 hours a week to outreach, including witnessing, follow-up, and conducting nightly fellowships. They also work up to 24 hours a week to support themselves.

When I went WOW, we had a three-day training session, learning how to apply Dale Carnegie techniques to witnessing. We were also taught how to undershepherd, a form of follow-up that continues until the trainee is able to witness and undershepherd someone himself. Is it any wonder that The Way is growing at a rapid rate?

On the last night of the WOW training, we were told where we would be spending the next year, and with whom. The next morning I left for Muncie, Indiana. If then, or later, I had felt I should be somewhere else, I would have been accused of questioning "the revelation" received by Dr. Wierwille.

At no time are followers of The Way encouraged to seek God's will for their lives. Decisions are always made for them. Once I wanted to take two majors in college. When I sought validation from my leader, he thundered, "Forget it! If God wants to tell you anything, He'll tell me first."

Sexual exploitation is visible in The Way, although it is not widespread. Leaders can pick and choose, and it would be a terrible faux pas to refuse a person in the higher echelons of leadership. Sex has occasionally been used as a recruitment tool.

When asked why I had not signed up a young man whom I was undershepherding for PFAL, I told the leader that I thought the young man was more interested in me than he was in PFAL. The leader ordered me to encourage him and use his interest in me as a tool to sign him up. I asked the leader if he wanted me to go to bed with the recruit to sign him up, and he replied, "Do whatever you have to do." Happily, in this case it was not required. If it had been, my blind loyalty to the organization would have led me to do it. Anything less would have been spiritual insubordination, and I would have been responsible for my disobedience.

Perhaps the most psychologically damaging aspect of becoming involved in The Way is the loss of self-identity. Career plans, marriage, or other major decisions must be cleared with the leadership. Everything is in terms of "the family" instead of the individual. On the surface, this appears to be dedication and spiritual maturity, but the priority is relationship to organization, not a personal relationship with Jesus Christ.

Doctrinal teaching also provides an effective way of alienating the individual from his former self, and in particular, from the organized church. Dr. Wierwille's "special discoveries" placed us a notch above other Christians. Revealed to him through his Bible study, they had to be true. And didn't God speak audibly to him? "The greatest man of God since the Apostle Paul" (by his evaluation) taught us several doctrinal teachings which were used to establish continuity and unity. After all, "we" know it; "they" don't.

The cardinal doctrine and a major heresy in The Way is the teaching expressed by the title of Dr. Wierwille's book *Jesus Christ is NOT God*. With blatancy, he declares that Jesus Christ is not God, never has been, and never will be. The Way teaches that the Father alone is God. Jesus Christ did not exist prior to His conception in Mary's womb, and there are only two factors which distinguish Him from any other man: He always walked in perfect fellowship with the Father and did the Father's will, and He had pure blood. The latter was accomplished, according to Dr. Wierwille, because God placed "divine sperm" in Mary's uterus when He overshadowed her "like a bull overshadows a cow."

Other doctrinal beliefs further indicate that The Way is spurious: Belief in the Trinity is a form of "spiritual whoredom" which can result in demon possession; the Holy Spirit is another name for God the Father, "like Bob is another name for Robert"; the cross is considered a pagan symbol of death; people in this administration (dispensation of grace) will not go to hell—at least Dr. Wierwille finds nothing in the Bible to indicate they will!

The Way teaches that the denominations are financing deprogramming. I believed that the organized church's primary goal was to hinder The Way. Dr. Wierwille repeatedly told us that we were the center of modern history, and that all of the major world crises were Satan's method of attacking The Way. We were taught that we were being persecuted and that the only way to maintain was to remain close to each other, and exclude all others. As early as 1973, there were conversations about measures that had to be taken "if we ever need to go underground." I have learned from an ex-member of The Way Corps that this rationale is a common reason given for the gestapolike training that exemplifies The Way Corps. With this psychology prevalent, it is not surprising that members of The Corps must take rifle-training courses in Emporia.

There came a time when I could no longer condone the sexual and financial exploitation or ignore the mental manipulation. No longer could I teach free will to prospects when I was undeniably in bondage to the overpowering organization. No longer could I push myself without adequate rest toward the goals of Word Over the World. Yet my options were extremely limited.

How does one walk out on "the greatest man of God since the Apostle Paul"? Where does one go when the only close associations of the past eight years have been with the group which you can no longer endure? How does one admit that eight years of life have been squandered in chasing a lie? Having found no better answer to these questions, I took the bottle of Darvon and lay down to die.

At first I felt an incredible sense of relief. I was no longer propagating something I didn't believe in. I no longer pretended to have all the answers to life. But I didn't care now; soon I would be a person of the past. However, a Power stronger than any pill or any circumstance was also present in that room, for obviously I did not die, nor even become ill. I had chosen Darvon with alcohol believing it would be lethal and would act slowly to give me time to change my mind should I want to back out and get medical help. But as I lay still for two hours, I became more confused and angry with every minute that passed. Finally I realized that God had to be behind what was happening. I screamed, "God, You already got eight years of my life. I refuse to go on like this! This is not living; this is hardly even existing." My tirade was followed by silence.

"God," I screamed, "I can't go on like this! Something has to change." I knew, as soon as I said it, that God did not want me to go on living a sham. Somewhere there was truth, and He would lead me to it.

"OK, God," I yelled, "I'll give You one year. That's all You have!" God looked past my impertinence and into my heart. He knew the hurt behind the anger, and the fear behind the bravado.

Defeated, yet hopeful, I checked out of the motel with no idea where to go next, except back to my roommates who belonged to The Way. Next day it occurred to me to phone Teen Challenge in Indianapolis. I had once attended a crusade conducted by David Wilkerson, founder of Teen Challenge, and felt that he was "for real." By "chance," the young woman I talked with had once been involved in The Way. She encouraged me to go to a church where I could find the truth and love to heal my emotional wounds.

This threatened me because I had been taught that the church was an enemy which was keeping us true believers under attack, and that I would find only hard, liturgical death within those stained-glass enclosures. Still, I had to admit that God had worked in some incredible ways in the past hours. If this was the next step, then I must take it. I picked the First Assembly of God of Speedway, Indiana from the listing in the yellow pages.

Entering the church that Sunday evening was one of the most frightening experiences of my life. I arrived after the service had started and sat in the back row. At the closing "amen" I was almost out the door, but three people intercepted me to say they were glad I had come.

The next day I made an appointment to see the minister, the Rev. Thomas Bell. He had never heard of The Way, causing me to realize the churches were not out to "get" The Way. He welcomed me to attend the church, dispelling my belief that the church considered us as spiritual pariahs.

The most important factor in my reintegration was the love of God shown to me by the people in the church. I found that this love pointed past a human leader to a vital relationship with Jesus

Christ, the Incarnate Word.

Yet the transition was the most difficult period of my life. Often I felt racking guilt, wondering if I really had walked out on "the greatest man of God since the Apostle Paul." I told God that I was incapable of figuring it all out. I trusted Him to reveal Himself to me; I wanted His truth. I am convinced that God had been waiting to hear that.

As I have developed a personal relationship with Jesus Christ, He has healed the hurts, the distrust, and fears. He has given me ability to identify with hurting people, especially those in the cults.

The Lord has healed me of the intense bitterness that I had toward The Way. There is a strong delusion prevalent there, Satanic in origin. I do not believe that Dr. Wierwille is "on the take"; I believe that he is sincere, and may be under a stronger delusion than anyone else in The Way. But, as he himself has said, "You can be sincerely wrong." The dedication that is prevalent in The Way, if rechanneled, could be a tremendous addition to the church. It would mean loving ex-cultists who wouldn't be capable of loving you in return for a while, and applying God's love as a healing ointment to wounds that have festered for years. The alternative is to let those wounds fester, to let the people who leave the cults remain with only the broken bubble of a once viable dream. As Christ's ambassadors, can we really do that?

A few months ago, I left Indiana for the best reason that I can imagine. I returned to my hometown to prepare to enter Bible college. God has fulfilled my desire beyond my wildest dream. Instead of putting me on a shelf as "unfit," He has called me into His service. At this point, I don't know exactly what ministry, but God will lead me step by step.

Perhaps God will lead me into a counseling ministry to aid people who need direction and love as they try to put their lives back together. I would welcome working with ex-cultists. I have a substantial library of books on cults, including *Know the Marks of Cults* by David Breese [see chapter 19]. I count this book one of the most valuable because it teaches how to be aware of characteristics common to cults. This book helped me tremendously in the months following my break with The Way.

As I look to the future, no matter how tough the going, God will never let me down. No easy answers, no quick claims, but He is omniscient, and His wisdom is far greater than mine.

Darkness vs. Light

The Way Says:

"Jesus Christ was with God before the foundation of the world, meaning that God foreknew him. . . . When Jesus Christ was born, he came into existence. Foreknowledge became a reality." (Victor Wierwille, *Jesus Christ Is Not God*)

"He spoke to me audibly, just like I'm talking to you now. He said He would teach me the Word as it had not been known since the first century if I would teach it to others. Well, I nearly flew off my chair. I couldn't believe that God would talk to me." (Victor Wierwille, in *The Way: Living in Love*, by Elena S. Whiteside)

"Gravedom . . . is a place where there is no consciousness and thus no remembrance." (Victor Wierwille, *Are the Dead Alive Now?*)

"They [the Father and the Son] are not 'coeternal, without beginning or end, and coequal.'" (Victor Wierwille, *Jesus Christ Is Not God*)

The Bible Says:

"You are from below. I am from above." / "Before Abraham was born, I AM." (Jesus, *John* 8:23, 58) / "All things came into being by Him [Christ]." (Apostle John, *John* 1:3)

"When a prophet speaks in the name of the Lord, if the thing does not come about or come true, that is the thing which the Lord has not spoken. The prophet has spoken it presumptuously." (Jehovah, *Deuteronomy* 18:22)

"I saw underneath the altar the souls of those who had been slain because of the Word of God . . . and they cried out with a loud voice, saying, 'How long, O Lord, holy and true, wilt Thou refrain from judging and avenging our blood?'" (Apostle John, *Revelation* 6:9-10)

"Thus says the Lord, the King of Israel, 'I am the first and I am the last, and there is no God besides Me." (Jehovah, *Isaiah* 44:6) / "Behold, I am coming quickly, and My reward is with Me. . . . I am the Alpha and the Omega . . . the beginning and the end." (Jesus, *Revelation* 22:12-13)

3
I Was a False Witness

by William Cetnar

I was almost a year old when two Jehovah's Witnesses came knocking at our door in Ambridge, Pennsylvania. The group had just officially changed its name, based on Isaiah 43:10: "'Ye are My witnesses,' saith the Lord [Jehovah]" (KJV).

Before that time, these door-to-door evangelists were called "Russellites" after their founder, Charles Taze Russell, a Congregational church member who didn't accept orthodox Christianity—particularly its teaching about eternal punishment for rejecters of Christ. Russell incorporated the Watchtower Bible and Tract Society in 1884 to spread his beliefs.

My parents, disillusioned Roman Catholics, weren't particularly interested in this history, but gradually they were drawn to these friendly callers who convinced them they represented God's theocratic organization on earth. Soon my father became the first presiding JW minister in our town, and I grew up being taught two basic principles that all JWs believe: (1) the Bible is God's book, inspired and to be obeyed, and (2) Bethel, the Watchtower Society at 124 Columbia Heights, Brooklyn, New York, is God's visible

---

William Cetnar is a stockbroker and heads the Ex-Jehovah's Witnesses for Jesus organization, R.D. 3, Kunkletown, PA 18058.

theocratic organization; whatever word comes from the Watchtower is equal to Scripture.

I also learned that since the fall into sin by Adam and Eve, God's sovereignty had been cast aside, and chosen servants must aid Him in restoring His rightful rule. Already, most of the highest elect, 144,000 to be exact, were reigning with Jesus—who, though not God, had died as a human sacrifice for man's sins. Any JWs after 1935—the "other sheep"—would eventually be rewarded with a paradise on earth, but status depended on works—a JW cornerstone.

At age 11 I sincerely wanted to serve Jehovah, and I was baptized at a Detroit convention. Someday I hoped to work with the leaders at Bethel. There men served God faithfully in celibacy for $14 a month.

As a youth, I thought I could best serve by being an attorney who represented JWs. After all, we were getting hauled into court and prison often those days. Resisting as idol worship any authority other than Jehovah, we would not salute the American flag, sing the national anthem, vote, or serve in the armed forces. My parents were jailed for carrying on their car the JW sign, "Religion Is a Snare and a Racket."

But my law plans were thwarted under the influence of Missouri Judge Joseph Franklin Rutherford, who succeeded founder Russell as president from 1917-1942. Judge Rutherford, who never finished high school and who never was officially appointed a judge, convinced me there was no time for law school; I should set my sights on the Watchtower. With JW zeal I served four years as a "summer pioneer," putting in 150 hours a month going door-to-door and publicizing our park meetings. Occasionally a person would ask if I had been "born again." I replied, "Yes," and thought to myself, "Now let's talk about something important."

At age 18, I became a full-time pioneer and was assigned to Beverly Hills, where I met several motion picture celebrities. I started Bible studies among some of those well-known people. Later I was transferred to Pacific Grove.

In 1950, President Nathan Homer Knorr (1942-1977) invited me to work inside my Brooklyn mecca as a waiter. A year later I graduated to the Service Department and was elated to answer Bible questions from letter writers.

But the grandeur was altered from the inside. My vision dimmed with one of the first letters. A young lady in Texas wrote, "Is it really a violation of God's law to have a smallpox vaccination?"

Actually, there was a "yes-it-is" standard reply letter already printed, but as similar letters came in, I had my doubts. For 30 years the Watchtower had taught that this vaccination violated God's law of not drinking blood, based on Acts 15. During World War II and afterward when JWs went to prison for pacifism, they were thrown into solitary confinement for refusing to take the inoculations.

I decided to visit a pharmaceutical laboratory where smallpox vaccine was made. After getting the tour, I was still puzzled. "Where is the cow's blood from which you make the smallpox vaccine?" The New Jersey officials smiled at my question. They did not know of anyone who used cow's blood in the vaccine.

I returned to headquarters and wrote a memo to President Knorr. He never officially answered it, but "God changed his mind" on April 14, 1952! After that a new letter, permitting the vaccine, was sent out.

From boyhood, I had been taught that God, via angels, communicated His will to the JW president. But at Bethel I learned something else. Whenever I couldn't find an answer for a question, it was Vice-President F.W. Franz, not the aged president, who clarified the matter.

But Knorr had some ideas of his own on divine revelation. One day in an editorial meeting, we got into a heated discussion about what we should publish. Knorr jumped up from the table and said, "You fellas can argue about this all you want, but when you get it argued out and it comes off the sixth floor, it will be the truth."

So it was that during my more than eight years at headquarters, most decisions were hashed out by underlings, but once they were printed, they became God's truth.

There were many other discrepancies which ate at my conscience. Knorr forbade marriage at headquarters—that is, until 1953, when he decided to marry. Afterward it was strongly encouraged.

Also, JWs were not considered members in good standing unless they did monthly door-to-door field service. But I observed that many Watchtower leaders did not hit the blocks. Instead, they had a ruling that speaking at weddings and funerals counted as field service time.

Another incident which bothered me happened right after I was given the responsibility of handling the rental of the JW apartments across the street from Bethel. After I rented the first apartment to a black couple, Knorr told me he would not permit them residency, and in the future I should not rent to blacks. This was strange in a religion where brother and sister equality appeals to many blacks.

Then there was the issue of blood transfusions—a life-and-death JW judgment. JWs to this day do not permit transfusions, and almost every year the media cover cases where people die from not accepting this treatment. The transfusion taboo came out strongly in 1952, though a few JW articles on the subject had been printed as early as 1944. I searched for a biblical basis for this ban and concluded it was not a sin. I then refused to write letters advising people to abstain from the treatment. Even the editor of the JW *Awake* magazine did not believe transfusions violated God's law, and he would have accepted a transfusion if necessary. Yet he wrote articles forbidding it because of pressures from the top.

The refusal to write such letters resulted in my move from the sixth floor to the JW reception desk. Leaders hoped I would come to my senses, and therefore I still was allowed to give speeches for our "united" cause.

At the reception desk I met a visitor, Walter R. Martin, author of *The Kingdom of the Cults,* who planted a seed of truth when he asked me to read Isaiah 44:6 where Jehovah declares that "there is no God besides Me." Since Jehovah is the only God, how could JWs say the *Logos* ("Jesus") is a lesser god? Martin challenged. It was one of the unraveling threads in my religion.

I gave my last JW speech to a quarter million faithful in Yankee Stadium in July 1958. Shortly afterward the tensions finally resulted in my headquarters resignation. My fiancée, Joan, a Bethel worker for four years, also resigned. When we married, we lived next door to her parents and still participated in the local JW Kingdom Hall on a lay level.

My inevitable "disfellowship" for apostasy came in December 1962. I advised a couple to let their doctor determine if their granddaughter needed a blood transfusion. I was excommunicated. The tension in our JW community over my stance resulted in our move to California, where a friend offered me work as a painter.

Not knowing who Jesus really is, I began to research Scripture and the Watchtower's older publications to unscramble my contradicting faith. In JW material I discovered many false prophecies. Our leaders had received messages from God that the world would end in 1874, 1879, 1881, 1914, 1918, 1925, and 1941. (Even in 1980 one issue of the *Watchtower* apologized for disappointing so many people by announcing 1975 as the end-of-the-world date.) I realized my disenchantment was not with just a few men but with an organization that printed lies and false doctrine. Jesus' words suddenly hit me with new force: "Watch out for false prophets. They come to you in sheep's clothing, but inwardly they are ferocious wolves. By their fruit you will recognize them" (Matthew 7:15-16, NIV).

As Joan's and my disillusionment with the JWs increased, we became more open to other avenues. A local minister asked me to speak on "JWs and blood transfusions" at his church. The talk and Joan's presence there resulted in a JW hearing for Joan by the judicial committee in Santa Ana to determine if she should be disfellowshiped. The publicity of that hearing resulted in a news article in the local *Register*. That story brought us into contact with other ex-Jehovah's Witnesses and Christians who helped us study materials to understand that Jesus was more than Michael the archangel: He was and is Yahweh—the same One who said, "I AM" to Moses in the burning bush.

For us it was a coming home to truth. We were baptized as born-again believers in 1964. Our profession resulted in losing ties with many friends and family members, including Joan's parents, but we stand firmly committed to the Lord Jesus Christ, the Shepherd who can discern wolves in sheep's clothing.

Darkness vs. Light

Jehovah's Witnesses Say:

"Our Redeemer existed as a spirit being before he was made flesh and dwelt amongst men. At that time, as well as subsequently, he was properly known as 'a god'—a mighty one. As chief of the angels and next to the Father, he was known as the Archangel (highest angel or messenger), whose name, Michael, signifies 'Who as God,' or God's representative." (Charles Taze Russell, *Studies In The Scriptures, Volume V*)

"Only the religious 'trinitarians' are presumptuous enough to claim, without Scripture basis, that two other persons are equal with Jehovah God; but Jesus does not himself claim to be one of such persons." (*The Kingdom Is at Hand*, Watch Tower Bible and Tract Society)

"You must love Jehovah's universal sovereignty . . . you must uphold it and proclaim it and remain true to it at all costs until it is vindicated. Only then may you survive Armageddon." (*You May Survive Armageddon Into God's New World*, W. T. B. & T. S.)

"It is so plain that the Bible hell is the tomb, the grave, that even an honest little child can understand it, but not the religious theologians." (*Let God Be True*, W. T. B. & T. S.)

The Bible Says:

"To which of the angels did He ever say, 'Thou are My Son'?" / And of the angels He says, 'Who makes His angels winds, and His ministers a flame of fire.' But of the Son He says, 'Thy throne, O God, is forever and ever.'" (*Hebrews* 1:5, 7-8)

"The grace of the Lord Jesus Christ, and the love of God, and the fellowship of the Holy Spirit, be with you all." / "Through Him (Christ) we both have our access in one Spirit to the Father." (Apostle Paul, *2 Corinthians* 13:14; *Ephesians* 2:18)

"This is My Son, My Chosen One; listen to Him." (Jehovah, *Luke* 9:35) / "He who hears My word, and believes Him who sent Me, has eternal life, and does not come into judgment, but has passed out of death into life." (Jesus, *John* 5:24)

"The poor man died and he was carried . . . to Abraham's bosom. The rich man also died and was buried; and in Hades . . . being in torment . . . he cried out . . . 'I am in agony in this flame.'" (Jesus, *Luke* 16:22-24)

I Was a False Witness / 37

"Who, and how many, are able to enter the Kingdom? Revelation limits the number to 144,000 that become a part of the Kingdom and stand on Mount Zion." (*Let God Be True*, W. T. B. & T. S.)

"I heard the number of those who were sealed, one hundred and forty-four thousand sealed from every tribe of the sons of Israel." / "After these things I looked, and behold, a great multitude, which no one could count, from every nation and all tribes and peoples and tongues, standing before the throne and before the Lamb . . . saying, 'Salvation to our God.'" (Apostle John, *Revelation* 7:4, 9-10)

"Since no earthly men have ever seen the Father . . . neither will they see the glorified Son." (*Let God Be True*, W. T. B. & T. S.)

"Men of Galilee, why do you stand looking into the sky? This Jesus, who has been taken up from you into heaven, will come in just the same way as you have watched Him go into heaven." (Angels, *Acts* 1:11) / "He is coming with the clouds, and every eye will see Him." (Apostle John, *Revelation* 1:7)

"The undefeatable purpose of Jehovah God to establish a righteous kingdom in these last days was fulfilled A.D. 1914." (*Let God Be True*, W. T. B. & T. S.) / "Christ Jesus came to the Kingdom in A.D. 1914, but unseen to men." (*The Truth Shall Make You Free*, W. T. B. & T. S.)

"Just as the lightning comes from the east and flashes even to the west, so shall the coming of the Son of man be. And then all the tribes of the earth will mourn, and they will see the Son of Man coming on the clouds." (Jesus, *Matthew* 24:27, 30) / "Jesus shall be revealed from heaven with His mighty angels in flaming fire, dealing out retribution." (Apostle Paul, *2 Thessalonians* 1:7-8)

4
In and Out of Mormonism

*By Marolyn Wragg
as told to Roger F. Campbell*

Shortly before we moved to the twin cities of Benton Harbor and St. Joseph, Michigan, I stopped attending the Baptist church in our town. The most convenient excuse was the arrival of another baby at our house.

There had been a time when the church had been important to me. I had professed Christ as my Saviour at a youth rally not long after my twelfth birthday. I had gone home that night with a burning desire to live for the Lord. I'd greatly enjoyed studying the Bible, memorizing its verses, and singing the hymns and choruses of the church.

Time passed quickly. The year of our move to St. Joseph found me the mother of four children. Our move came as a result of my husband's new teaching position in the twin-city school system.

It was exciting to move into our new home. The community warmly welcomed us. Everything seemed to be nearly perfect—everything except my relationship to God. We were not attending

---

Marolyn E. Wragg is a homemaker who resides near Muskegon, Michigan. *The Rev. Roger F. Campbell* is a former pastor who travels widely for speaking engagements and spends much time in a free-lance writing ministry. He resides in Waterford, Michigan.

church, and my Bible had become a neglected book.

From time to time I thought of attending church services, but I reasoned that I didn't know where to go, or that I didn't want to pick the wrong church.

When two Mormon missionaries first knocked at our door, I had been out of regular contact with any church for more than a year. They asked if they might have a few minutes of my time to "discuss the gospel." The "few minutes" grew into about one and a half hours, and in those 90 minutes I found myself fascinated with the statements of the Mormons. When they asked if they could return the following week for another "discussion," I eagerly accepted.

Though after the first visit, I counted the experience as just a good opportunity to learn the teaching of another religion, the next three months found me devouring Mormon literature. I read *The Book of Mormon, The Doctrine and Covenants,* and *The Pearl of Great Price,* in addition to several pamphlets and books written by authorities of the Mormon Church.

Within three months, the Mormons convinced me that Joseph Smith was indeed a prophet of God and the instrument through which God had restored the gospel in its fullness. I was baptized into the Church of Jesus Christ of Latter-Day Saints, with the intention of influencing my family and friends to become Mormons.

I put forth every effort to lead our children into my new church. Our two oldest boys, then 8 and 10, were soon eligible for baptism, for, according to Mormon teaching, the age of accountability is 8 years.

Later, when they were 12, they were ordained deacons in the Aaronic priesthood, and at 14 the eldest was ordained a teacher in that priesthood. I was proud and pleased.

My responsibilities and involvement continued to increase. I became the regular teacher of the adult Sunday School class, and also served as a relief society visiting teacher.

During my first years in LDS, I was constantly fascinated with the answers that Mormon writings gave to questions that I had always pondered. Most comforting of all was the Mormon teaching on baptism for the dead. If any of my loved ones should die without turning to Christ, I would not need to be too concerned, for there would be further opportunities after this life, and I could be baptized on their behalf.

My desire to understand all the doctrines of the church led me to study ever more deeply the teaching of the Mormons. Then I began to see discrepancies between the simple Gospel of the Bible and the complex "gospel" of Mormonism.

The very teachings that at first had been so "fascinating" I now found frustrating. It seemed that every time I opened my Bible, such verses as these would leap out at me to refute the doctrines I had embraced:

"For I determined not to know any thing among you, save Jesus Christ and Him crucified" (1 Corinthians 2:2, KJV). "Who hath saved us and called us with an holy calling, not according to our works, but according to His own purpose and grace, which was given us in Christ Jesus before the world began" (2 Timothy 1:9, KJV). "Not by works of righteousness which we have done but according to His mercy He saved us" (Titus 3:5, KJV).

If I had never known anything better, perhaps I could have been satisfied with Mormonism, but once having known Christianity, I could not stay content with "religion." The little chorus "Something Happened When He Saved Me" kept running through my mind. Though I was still not ready to turn away from Mormonism, I had to admit that something had happened that night in my youth, and I could not make that experience fit into my understanding of my present religion. I tried to explain to myself that I had not gone deep enough into the Mormon faith, and so I continued to search the Mormon scriptures and to work harder to fulfill my duties in the church.

At this point I began to desire to attend a Gospel service in a church such as I had known in the past. I found myself longing to join in the singing of familiar hymns and to hear a message entirely from the Bible.

When Mrs. Barsuhn came to my door, it was to discuss my furnace. Before she left, we had discussed faith, and she invited me to attend the services of the Calvary Bible Church of Benton Harbor. She even offered to stop for me on the way so we could attend the service together.

My visit to an evening church service was the first of several. I was by no means ready to abandon my Mormon beliefs, but I did find the services enjoyable, and I reasoned that perhaps someday these people would come to understand and accept the "rest of the truth" held by the Church of Jesus Christ of Latter-Day Saints.

Eventually, however, I found myself in greater conflict of soul than ever. It became necessary to spend days in study to bolster my faith in Mormonism.

Making matters more difficult, nearly everything I read in the Bible seemed to deny rather than defend my beliefs as a Mormon. I remember especially the day I turned to Galatians 1:8 and read: "But though we, or an angel from heaven, preach any other Gospel unto you than that which we have preached unto you, let him be accursed" (KJV). I thought of Joseph Smith's alleged interview with the angel which Mormons claim brought about the writing of the *Book of Mormon*. I tried desperately to put the application out of my mind. How could I forsake these beliefs I had nurtured for five years? What kind of reaction would an "about face" bring in my family and friends? I struggled with these questions and became more miserable each day.

On the last Sunday in August 1965, I experienced one of my frequent urges to attend a Gospel service. That night I chose to visit the North Lincoln Baptist Church of St. Joseph. Pastor Weiss of that church had called in my home and I had appreciated his sincerity. As I made my way home after the service, I felt guilty for having so much enjoyed a service in a Baptist church. That didn't seem proper for a Mormon Sunday School teacher.

Sleep eluded me that night. I could not rest with so many important questions unanswered. Of one thing I became certain: I could not continue in such an unsettled state. I felt that I had to know what to do that very week, and I prayed that God would show me what He would have me to do.

On Wednesday afternoon of my "week of decision," a telephone call came from Pastor Roger Campbell of the Calvary Bible Church in Benton Harbor. I had not heard from him for some time and concluded that he had given up hope of leading me out of Mormonism. He informed me that his church was having a missionary to the Mormons as a speaker that evening. He asked if I would consider coming, and to visit with him and the speaker afterward.

I wondered, as I held the telephone in my hand, if this call was the answer to my prayer. I thanked the pastor, and I determined that if it were at all possible, I would be at that meeting.

As I listened to Richard Manion of Pocatello, Idaho tell of his witness among the Mormons, I felt the Mormon defenses that I had been building for five years moving into action. I took notes on his presentation, intending to refute some of the things he was saying in our visit after the meeting.

In the visit that followed, I found that Mr. Manion and Pastor Campbell were able to answer some of my questions. They discussed several doctrines of the Mormon Church and pointed out Bible verses that dealt with these doctrines. I noticed especially that they kept steering the conversation back to the way of salvation. They insisted that no one could have peace with God unless his salvation was based on God's grace through faith in Christ. They urged me to read the Gospel of John and the Book of Romans, in which they felt I would find the answers I so earnestly sought.

I went home to another experience of struggling and searching. During the night, I read the entire Book of Romans, and once again I faced the dilemma of seeing my beliefs seemingly contradicted by the plain statements of the Bible. I could find no way to escape the clear teaching of Romans 4:5: "But to him that worketh not, but believeth on Him that justifieth the ungodly, his faith is counted for righteousness" (KJV).

The light was beginning to break through. I had asked the Lord to end my search for truth that week. The telephone call from Pastor Campbell had come on Wednesday. Wednesday evening had brought my meeting with the missionary, followed by hours in the Book of Romans. This called for another counseling session on Thursday. On Friday I studied a book written by William Biederwolf entitled *Mormanism under the Searchlight*.

As I read Biederwolf's analysis of the history and doctrines of Mormonism, as compared with the Bible, my remaining questions were answered. I had no more doubts as to what I should do. A great load had been lifted from me.

I knelt to pray to my Saviour. As I prayed, I experienced the wonderful forgiveness of Christ, and I felt once again the peace and joy that comes from trusting fully in Jesus Christ as Lord and Saviour.

As I rose from my knees, I knew I faced many difficult tasks, not the least being resigning from my duties in the Mormon Church. I felt sure that Christ would give me the strength to accomplish anything He wanted me to do.

I was right! Christ has been sufficient for me in every situation.

In fact, realizing the sufficiency of Christ has become one of my greatest blessings.

My five years as a Mormon taught me many lessons. I know now the importance of regular attendance in a Bible-teaching church, and of diligent Bible study to keep from being "tossed to and fro . . . with every wind of doctrine" (Ephesians 4:14, KJV). I know how vital it can be to witness to those who are caught in error, as others took time to witness to me. I know too that it pays to pray for those in need of spiritual help, for I discovered that many were praying for me.

As a result of these years, I also want the many sincere people in Mormonism to have something far greater than "religion." To all Mormons who read my story, I direct these vital words from the Bible: "For by *grace* you have been *saved* through *faith;* and that not of yourselves, it is the gift of God; not as a result of works, that no one should boast. Therefore having been justified by *faith,* we have peace with God through our Lord Jesus Christ" (Ephesians 2:8-9; Romans 5:1, emphasis that of author).

Darkness vs. Light

Mormons Say:

"In the heaven where our spirits were born, there are many Gods, each of whom has his own wife, or wives, which were given to him previous to his redemption, while yet in his mortal state." (Orson Pratt, *The Seer*)

"Jesus Christ was a polygamist; Mary and Martha, the sisters of Lazarus, were his plural wives, and Mary Magdalene was another." (Brigham Young, *Wife Number 19*)

"The sectarian dogma of justification by faith alone has exercised an influence for evil since the early days of Christianity." (James Talmage, *Articles of Faith*)

"The false doctrine that the punishment to be visited upon erring souls is endless, that every sentence for sin is of interminable duration, must be regarded as one of the most pernicious results of misapprehension of Scripture." (James Talmage, *Articles of Faith,* 1941 edition)

The Bible Says:

"The sons of this age marry and are given in marriage, but those who are considered worthy to attain to that age and the resurrection from the dead, neither marry nor are given in marriage . . . and are like angels." (Jesus, *Luke* 20:34-36)

"The foxes have holes, and the birds of the air have nests, but the Son of man has nowhere to lay His head." / "There are eunuchs who were born that way . . . and there are also eunuchs who made themselves eunuchs for the sake of the kingdom of heaven. He who is able to accept this, let him accept it." (Jesus, *Luke* 9:58; *Matthew* 19:12)

"This is the work of God, that you believe in Him whom He has sent." (Jesus, *John* 6:29) / "To the one who does not work, but believes in Him who justifies the ungodly, his faith is reckoned for righteousness." (Apostle Paul, *Romans* 4:5)

"He who believes in the Son has eternal life; but he who does not obey the Son shall not see life, but the wrath of God abides on him." (John the Baptist, *John* 3:36)

In and Out of Mormonism / 45

"As man is, God once was; as God is, man may become." (Lorenzo Snow, *Instructor,* December 1938)

"The people of the last days profess to have the Priesthood of the Almighty; the power to act in the name of God, which power commands respect both on earth and in heaven." (James Talmage, *Articles of Faith*)

"Present and continuous revelation from God to the Church through its earthly head, and to every member who seeks for it in his or her own behalf and guidance, is a fundamental principle of the 'Mormon' faith." (Charles Penrose, *What The Mormons Believe*)

"O candidates for celestial glory! Would you, like your heavenly Father, prompted by eternal benevolence and charity, wish to fill countless millions of worlds with your begotten sons and daughters and to bring them all through the gradations of progressive being, to inherit immortal bodies and eternal mansions in your several dominions?" (Parley P. Pratt, *Key To The Science of Theology,* 9th edition)

"I am the first, and I am the last, and there is no God besides Me." / "I, the Lord, do not change." (Jehovah, *Isaiah* 44:6; *Malachi* 3:6)

"All authority has been given to Me in heaven and on earth." (Jesus, *Matthew* 28:18)/"There is one God and one mediator also between God and men, the man Christ Jesus." (Apostle Paul, 1 *Timothy* 2:5)

"I testify to everyone who hears the words of the prophecy of this book: if anyone adds to them, God shall add to him the plagues which are written in this book. And if anyone takes away from the words of the book of this prophecy, God shall take away his part from the tree of life and from the holy city." (Apostle John, *Revelation* 22:18-19)

"Certain persons have crept in . . . ungodly persons who turn the grace of our God into licentiousness and deny our only Master and Lord, Jesus Christ." (Jude, *Jude* 1:4) / "You shall worship the Lord your God and serve Him only." (Jesus, *Matthew* 4:10)

5
Why I Left Christian Science

by Carolyn Poole

As I sit at my desk before an open window that lets in a gentle breeze, I hold in my hand a letter from a woman who follows the teaching of Christian Science.

Her letter begins: "I would appreciate some information on your 'alternative' to Christian Science. I am a class-taught Scientist who has been a member of the church for about 12 years. I must confess, however, coming from a traditional Protestant background as I do, that many of the points you bring up are the ones that have troubled me, but the good always seemed to far outweigh these troublesome points, which I chose to ignore. I guess my main problem is now that I have progressed to this point, I cannot imagine an alternative to Christian Science. I will be interested to hear how others are handling this."

As I read her words, I feel the questioning, the searching that she is going through. I don't know much about her, but maybe my answer to her letter will make the difference for her for all eternity. So taking pen in hand, I go back in memory to tell her of my own journey out of Christian Science.

Carolyn Poole is a homemaker who is director of the Christian Way, associated with the United Evangelical Churches. Her address is P.O. Box 1675, Lancaster, CA 93534.

Why I Left Christian Science / 47

Christian Science was the most important thing in my life. I had been born and reared in it. I was a third-generation member of the church and I too was class taught. I faithfully served on most of the committees and as president of our executive board. I relied totally on Christian Science, neither going to doctors nor taking medicine. I truly loved my religion and expected to be a loyal Scientist for the rest of my life.

Something happened to change my thinking. I believe that the best way for me to explain it is to tell my story in the sequence that it occurred.

In 1975, while I was president of the executive board in a small branch church, I felt a need to know the Bible better. I believed that my religion was based on the Bible, and regarded the Bible as one of our two pastors. I realized, however, that in getting my daily lessons, I was not reading much of the Bible. So I proposed to the church that we have a Bible study following a certain Christian Scientist's teaching on cassette tapes. Nothing came of it.

It was during this same time that two women came to my front door and invited me to attend the Christian Women's Club home Bible studies. I cautiously accepted. At first I didn't see anything different in these studies except that the women were the sweetest and nicest I had ever met. I felt "good" in their company.

After a few months a Bible verse loomed up to disturb my thinking. My husband was reading to me: "Nor should you be called 'Leader,' because your one and only leader is the Messiah" (Matthew 23:10, TEV). It was Jesus speaking. This caused both of us to sit up and take notice, because Mrs. Eddy and Jesus were each claiming to be our only leader. You can't have two leaders.

A couple of months later I found myself concerned about Mrs. Eddy being frequently referred to as "our revered Leader." I looked up that word *revered,* and found that two of its synonyms are *adore* and *worship.* I knew the Bible said that God is a jealous God who will not share His glory with anyone. I did not think that we should adore and worship anyone but God. I felt that it was sacrilegious to call Mrs. Eddy "our revered Leader."

A short while later, we started in our home a new study in the Gospel of John. This was when verses which I had read for years took on new meanings. It was as if I had never seen them before. They began to make an impact on my mind.

To start with, there were the words of Jesus, "I am the way, the truth, and the life; no one comes to the Father, but through Me" (John 14:6).

This reminded me of what I had read in Christian Science that Mrs. Eddy is called the "Revelator" and that Christian Science is the "Revelation." We had been taught that you could not know the Revelation without knowing the Revelator. And, of course, we had to know the Revelation in order to properly understand God, so we had to know Mrs. Eddy in order to know God. This meant that, according to Christian Science, she is the way to God.

Jesus and Mrs. Eddy were, once again, making the same claim, that each was the way to God. I had the distinct impression that she had taken the place of Jesus in the minds of her followers.

Something else began appearing in my Bible reading. At first I could hardly believe it. I started seeing repeatedly, especially in the Gospel of John, that in order for us to have eternal life we must believe on Jesus. The Scriptures finally got through to me that we will perish if we don't accept Jesus. As I saw this word *perish*, I thought of hell, and hell was a condition I'd never believed in, except as a state of mind.

But the Bible said we would be eternally lost if we did not believe on Jesus. I hated the idea of anyone going to hell, but no matter how I felt about it, Jesus had said it. I realized that if it were true, it would be more unfortunate if Jesus hadn't warned people about eternal damnation. I learned that He spoke of hell many times. Could I believe that a good God could allow such a condition to exist? Well, I didn't make the rules, and God didn't ask me. God said, "For My thoughts are not your thoughts, neither are your ways My ways" (Isaiah 55:8).

Christian Science flatly contradicted what Jesus said about the state of our eternal existence. Up until then, I had always skipped past Jesus' references to hell, thinking He was speaking in a parable and that Mrs. Eddy's spiritual interpretation explained it all. It suddenly occurred to me, as chills ran up and down my spine, that maybe the Bible actually meant what it said.

I preferred what Mrs. Eddy said to what Jesus said—that there is no hell, no judgment day—but there was a serious problem in believing her. On thinking it out, I realized that she had never come back from the dead. She was only another mortal with a human father and mother. Her ideas about hell were her own. She wasn't qualified and I had been believing her to guide me in the matter of my eternal life. On the other hand Jesus was of virgin birth. His Father was God; He had risen from the dead. I thought of that familiar quotation, "What fools we mortals be!"

The Holy Spirit was working me over completely, because that wasn't all that broke open before my eyes. One day in Bible study we came to the part where Jesus asked His disciples who He was. As a Christian Scientist, I knew those verses by heart. So I recited, " 'Who do you say that I am?' and Simon Peter answered and said, 'Thou art the Christ, the Son of the living God.' " Jesus told Peter that "flesh and blood did not reveal this to you, but My Father who is in heaven" (Matthew 16:15-17).

In the days that followed, Jesus' question rang in my mind. It was as if Jesus was urgently asking me: "Who do you say that I am?" Peter had replied that Jesus is the Christ. Jesus and Christ are one and the same. Did I believe that? What did Mrs. Eddy say?

As I poured over her statements, it was apparent that she did not consider Jesus and Christ as one. Jesus merely demonstrated "the Christ idea." According to her, I could demonstrate the "Christ-Truth" as she termed it, as Jesus did. The only difference between Jesus and me was that Jesus was more advanced in His understanding, so He could demonstrate a higher reality.

I perceived another new concept about Jesus. Jesus, whom I had considered only to be the most perfect man, was called "God" in the Bible. In the Gospel of John, which I dearly loved as a Christian Scientist, I found "the Word was with God and the Word was God" (John 1:1) and a few lines farther "The Word became flesh" (1:14). In reverse, I saw that the flesh is Jesus, that Jesus is the Word, and that the Word [Jesus] is God. This meant Jesus is God.

Then there was Thomas who put his hand in Jesus' side and said, "My Lord and my God" (John 20:28). If Thomas was mistaken, Jesus would have quickly set him straight.

Also, consider how many times Jesus is called "Son of man" and other times "Son of God." Tie that in with His being conceived in a human mother by the Holy Spirit. Also, at the end of Jesus' earthly life, His body did not go back to dust as others do, but ascended to heaven. Mrs. Eddy's body went the way of all flesh.

The Apostle John warned of those who would deceive people about Jesus. He asked, "Who is the liar but the one who denies that Jesus is the Christ? This is the antichrist, the one who denies the Father and the Son" (1 John 2:22). It dawned on me who those "false prophets" are. They are the present-day religious leaders who take for themselves the place of Jesus, and who "mislead, if possible, even the elect" (Matthew 24:24). They are like the Pied Piper, leading mankind down a false trail into the kingdom of darkness.

It was a jolt when I discovered who is behind the lies and the false prophets. He is Satan. He is as real as God, and he is a power. He isn't an illusion, as Mrs. Eddy claimed. When she said there is no power apart from God, she was making me unaware of the enemy. Jesus said Satan is a liar, and the father of lies (John 8:44). Jesus also said, "I was watching Satan fall from heaven like lightning" (Luke 10:18). The Bible has many references to Satan. Nowhere is he called an illusion.

In addition, Mrs. Eddy said that man is sinless. If that were true, Jesus suffered on the cross for nothing. In fact, it would appear that Jesus was too stupid to know why He died. I cannot believe that Jesus was either stupid or a liar. He knew what He was saying and He meant it. The Apostle Paul said, "All have sinned and fall short of the glory of God" (Romans 3:23).

Suddenly one night in Bible study, pieces of the Bible came together for me. I remembered that in Revelation Jesus is called the Lamb. Then I remembered that He was crucified at the time of the Passover, and going back to the origin of the Passover, I found that the blood of an unblemished lamb was put on the doorposts to keep death out.

God instituted the offering of animals as a substitutionary sacrifice for the sins of man. This was continued until Jesus' blood was shed on the cross. As a Christian friend has since told me, "It is a crimson thread that runs through the Bible."

For a lifetime Christian Scientist, these facts were hard to accept, but I came to realize that Christian Science is diametrically opposed to the Bible. I found myself at the place where I had to take all of the Bible or none of it. As a Christian Scientist, I could not throw out the Bible, since I knew that God is real, that the spirit world is also real, that prayer works, and that I believed in Jesus—though only in a limited way. Then I came to the point where I had to accept Jesus' words concerning Himself and why He came, or I had to reject Him and the whole Bible. In either case I knew that Christian Science was wrong because it claimed to be based on the Bible, yet it denied its most basic doctrine.

I chose Jesus. I asked Him to forgive my sins, and to be my Lord and Saviour. I resigned from the Christian Science church. I now have the comforting knowledge that when I die I am going to be with Jesus Christ, forever.

Mrs. Eddy claimed that we need her book *Science and Health* to study with the Bible, but we read "No prophecy of Scripture is a matter of one's own interpretation" (2 Peter 1:20). We don't need Mrs. Eddy to interpret the Bible.

Also, the Holy Scriptures answer my question, "Why, Lord, do Christian Scientists not listen to the truth?" It is "because they [do] not receive the love of the truth, so as to be saved" (2 Thessalonians 2:10).

I pray that you will love the truth and thereby reject the darkness for the light of Jesus.

Darkness vs. Light

Christian Science Says:

"A Christian Scientist recognizes the fact that the diseased or sinful conditions are but false mesmeric states of consciousness, and he applies his understanding of divine Truth as the remedy." (Herman S. Hering, C.S.B., *Christian Science Healing: Spiritual and Scientific*)

"Man is incapable of sin, sickness, and death." (Mary Baker Eddy, *Science and Health With Key to the Scriptures*)

"No final judgment awaits mortals, for the judgment day of wisdom comes hourly and continually." (Mary Baker Eddy, *Science and Health*)

"The Christian believes that Christ is God . . . . Jesus Christ is not God." (Mary Baker Eddy, *Science and Health*)

"This Comforter I understand to be Divine Science." (Mary Baker Eddy, *Science and Health*)

The Bible Says:

"Then the Lord saw that the wickedness of man was great on the earth, and that every intent of the thoughts of his heart was only evil continually. And the Lord was sorry that He had made men on the earth." (Moses, *Genesis* 6:5-6)

"But each one is tempted when he is carried away and enticed by his own lust. Then when lust has conceived, it gives birth to sin; and when sin is accomplished, it brings forth death." (Apostle James, *James* 1:14-15)

"Follow the impulses of your heart and . . . know that God will bring you to judgment." (Solomon, *Ecclesiastes* 11:9) / "But the present heavens and earth by His word are being reserved for fire, kept for the day of judgment and destruction of ungodly men." (Apostle Peter, *2 Peter* 3:7)

"In the beginning was the Word, and the Word was with God, and the Word was God. And the Word became flesh and dwelt among us." (Apostle John, *John* 1:1, 14)

"If I go not away, the Comforter will not come unto you; but if I depart, I will send Him unto you. And when He is come, He will reprove the world of sin, and of righteousness, and of judgment." (Jesus, *John* 16:7-8, KJV)

Why I Left Christian Science / 53

"We acknowledge God's forgiveness of sin in the destruction of sin and the spiritual understanding that casts out evil as unreal." (Mary Baker Eddy, *Science and Health*)

"Sin and disease are figments of the mortal or carnal mind, to be destroyed, healed, by knowing their unreality." (Albert Field Gilmore, "Christian Science," in *Varieties of American Religion,* by Charles S. Braden)

"The heart is more deceitful than all else, and is desperately sick; who can understand it? I, the Lord, search the heart, I test the mind, even to give to each man according to his ways." (Jehovah, *Jeremiah* 17:9-10)

"If we say that we have no sin, we are deceiving ourselves, and the truth is not in us. If we confess our sins, He is faithful and righteous to forgive us our sins and to cleanse us from all unrighteousness." (Apostle John, *1 John* 1:8-9)

6
I Eluded Armstrong's Clutch

*by Joe Mehesy,
as told to Muriel Larson*

After graduating from Woodbridge (New Jersey) High School in the early 70's, I enrolled in Rutgers University. There I encountered a whole new world and began questioning the Roman Catholic religion in which I had been reared. "If a religion is to have any value," I thought, "it should make a difference in the lives of those who follow it. And I don't see that our religion has done that in the lives of our family and friends."

With this, I began to lose faith in my religion. Influenced by the teachings of evolution and the literature I had to read at college, I decided I could not know God even if He does exist. But sometimes in the night there would be a cry in my heart, "Oh, if there is a God, I wish I'd find Him and experience Him in my life!"

The following summer I heard a radio program called "The World Tomorrow." A man named Herbert W. Armstrong spoke as if he was very sure of himself. "The problem with Christianity today," he said, " is that it is built on the traditions of men and not on the Word of God, the Bible."

Joe Mehesy is married and serves as a missionary with Navajo Gospel Crusade, Cortez, Colorado. *Muriel Larson* is a free-lance writer who resides in Greenville, South Carolina.

"Hey, listen to that!" I exclaimed. "I have known there was something wrong with Christianity—maybe this fellow has the answer."

Though I would later discover that much of what he preached was untrue, he sounded convincing. In fact, he sounded so convincing that I went to a Bible bookstore in Perth Amboy, New Jersey the next weekend and bought a reference Bible. The proprietor, the Rev. Winston Hedberg, recognized my interest in spiritual things. As I spoke about Armstrong, however, he did not argue. Rather, he spoke about Jesus Christ and His death on Calvary for our sins. I thought this strange, for I believed that adhering to the right issues was all-important in the matter of religion.

I wrote to Herbert Armstrong for some of his literature and used it as a guide to study the Bible. I also listened regularly to his radio program. I was glad that I wasn't an agnostic anymore.

In fact, when I returned to Rutgers that fall as a sophomore, I felt that studying the Bible was more interesting than studying my major, biology. It occurred to me that it would be good to go to a school where I could study the Bible. Since Armstrong had a college in California, I thought maybe I could enroll there and become a student of the Bible.

When my parents separated that fall, it came as a shock. Yet their separation also became an incentive for me to carry out my plans. If I were to go to Armstrong's Ambassador College, I would need to earn some money, for my scholarship wouldn't transfer from Rutgers. I remained at Rutgers until the end of the first semester, intending to transfer eventually.

During that spring I often went to the Bible bookstore to buy interesting books, and each time, Mr. Hedberg spoke to me about Jesus. I also began to listen to WFME, a Christian radio station in Newark. Something about the way the broadcasts honored Jesus Christ appealed to me.

In my studies I became more confused about the different viewpoints concerning Bible doctrines. Each side gave verses to support its view. Deepening my despair was the conviction that I needed to know which religion is right and then follow that religion in order for my sins to be forgiven.

That spring I applied to Ambassador College for the following fall. "Perhaps I'll find out if Herbert Armstrong is really right by attending his school," I said hopefully. Anxiety and a sense of unworthiness increasingly gripped me. "Salvation *can't* be as complicated as it seems," I began to reason. "But how can I find it?"

One day early in July when I was at the Bible bookstore, Mr. Hedberg asked, "Do you have assurance of your salvation?" When I answered that I didn't, he quoted two Bible verses: "For God so loved the world, that He gave His only begotten Son, that whosoever believeth in Him should not perish, but have everlasting life" (John 3:16, KJV). "He that heareth My Word, and believeth on Him that sent Me, hath everlasting life, and shall not come into condemnation, but is passed from death unto life" (5:24).

"On the basis of those two verses," Mr. Hedberg said, "you can have that assurance."

I didn't see how salvation could be so simple. But when I got home I read a tract telling how the manager of radio station WFME had become a Christian. Some time later, while listening to my favorite program on that station, I heard a story that revealed the faith and personal relationship that some women had with Christ—how their prayers had been answered, and how they had been led daily by God.

Those women have something I do not have with all my Bible study, I thought. I read the tract again. I looked up John 3:16 and John 5:24 and read them. "He that believeth . . . hath everlasting life." *God is not asking me to understand,* I thought—*He's just asking me to believe!*

I knelt on the floor. "Lord," I prayed silently, "I cannot understand, but since You say it in Your Word, I believe it!" There I found new life in Christ. What joy, what relief, what a thrill to know that Jesus was my Saviour and I was forgiven of my sin!

Before accepting Christ, I had been confused by discrepancies between the views of Armstrong and evangelical Christian authors I had read. But now the Bible became an open book to me and, hungry for the truth, I drank it in. God's Spirit illuminated my understanding, and I had no trouble discerning the truth from error. I also could hardly wait to tell Pastor Hedberg how God had saved me. As I expected, he was overjoyed.

Mr. Hedberg then showed me the importance of church

attendance. With other believers, I could worship, enjoy Christian fellowship, and grow in my faith. I soon became a member of a Bible-believing church near home.

Not long after that, I enrolled at a Christian college in order to study the Bible and to learn how to serve God. I am now married to a fine Christian girl, and we are serving the Lord in Colorado as missionaries to the Navajo Indians.

Darkness vs. Light

Armstrongism Says:

"For two 19-year time cycles the original apostles did proclaim this gospel . . . but in A.D. 69 they fled. For 18 and one-half centuries that gospel was not preached. . . . Today Christ has raised up His work . . . preparation to His second coming . . . . "The World Tomorrow" and *The Plain Truth* are Christian instruments." (Herbert W. Armstrong, *The Inside Story of The World Tomorrow Broadcast*)

"The purpose of your being alive is that finally you be born into the kingdom of God, when you will actually be God, even as Jesus was and is God; and his Father, a different person, also is God. You are setting out in training to become Creator—to become God!" (H. W. Armstrong, *Why Were You Born?*)

"There is a 'spirit' in man (Job 32:8). But that spirit is not the man—and is not conscious apart from the man." (Garner Ted Armstrong, *When You Die—Then What Happens?*)

The Bible Says:

"There are some who are disturbing you, and want to distort the Gospel of Christ. But even though we, or an angel from heaven, should preach to you a Gospel contrary to that which we have preached to you, let him be accursed." (Apostle Paul, *Galatians* 1:7-8)

"He (Christ) has made us to be a kingdom, priests to His God and Father, to Him be the glory and the dominion forever and ever." (Apostle John, *Revelation* 1:6) / "Before Me there was no God formed, and there will be none after Me. I, even I, am the Lord; and there is no Saviour besides Me." (Jehovah, *Isaiah* 43:10-11)

"The dust will return to the earth as it was, and the spirit will return to God who gave it." (Solomon, *Ecclesiastes* 12:7)/"While we are at home in the body we are absent from the Lord . . . and prefer rather to be absent from the body and to be at home with the Lord." (Apostle Paul, *2 Corinthians* 5:6-8)

I Eluded Armstrong's Clutch / 59

"It is not only possible but obligatory—that we obey God's spiritual law, the *ten commandments,* as they are magnified throughout the Bible." (H. W. Armstrong, *The Plain Truth,* November, 1963)

"People have been taught, falsely, that 'Christ *completed* the plan of salvation on the Cross'—when actually it was only *begun* there. The popular denominations have taught, 'Just believe—that's all there is to it; believe on the Lord Jesus Christ, and you are that instant *saved!*'" (H. W. Armstrong, *All About Water Baptism*)

"The theologians and 'higher critics' have blindly accepted the heretical and false doctrine (introduced by pagan false prophets who crept in) that the Holy Spirit is a Third Person . . . . This limits God to three persons." (H. W. Armstrong, *The Plain Truth,* February 1962)

"As Lord of lords, Christ will begin to convert and save the entire world during His reign . . . all people will then come to know God. Their blindness and religious confusion will be removed and they will finally be converted." (H. W. Armstrong, *The Plain Truth,* October 1959)

"A man is not justified by the works of the Law but through faith in Christ Jesus." / "If righteousness comes through the Law, then Christ died needlessly." (Apostle Paul, *Galatians* 2:16, 21)

"By one offering He (Christ) has perfected for all time those who are sanctified." / "He saved us, not on the basis of deeds which we have done in righteousness, but according to His mercy, by the washing of regeneration and renewing by the Holy Spirit." (*Hebrews* 10:14; *Titus* 3:5)

"Whoever shall speak a word against the Son of man, it shall be forgiven him; but whoever shall speak against the Holy Spirit, it shall not be forgiven him, either in this age, or in the age to come." (Jesus, *Matthew* 12:32)

"I am the Alpha and the Omega, the beginning and the end. I will give to the one who thirsts from the spring of the water of life without cost . . . but for the cowardly and unbelieving and abominable and murderers and immoral persons and sorcerers and idolaters and all liars, their part will be in the lake that burns with fire and brimstone, which is the second death." (Apostle John, *Revelation* 21:6, 8)

7
I Was an Agnostic Unitarian
by Elizabeth Kanouse

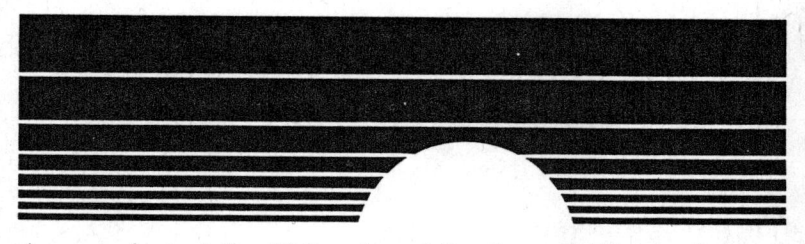

As a student at the University of Southern California, I was a debater, campus leader, and member of a sorority. But nothing satisfied me. I was often ill and was buffeted by waves of restlessness and discontent. A broken engagement engulfed me in despair.

Surrounded by effects of the nation's economic depression, I sought a cause that would bring hope to the world and give meaning to my life. My parents and maternal grandparents were socialists, so I absorbed their liberal views. My grandmother used to say she favored change through the ballot, not the bullet. But I was impatient and socialism was slow in coming. Curiosity led me to read the *Communist Manifesto* by Karl Marx and Friedrich Engels. Though Communism promised an immediate solution, it advocated an overthrow of the government. I concluded that a better world order could never be built on a foundation of enmity and strife, so I rejected Communism, and my search continued.

One of my debate partners persuaded me to attend a meeting of the local National Student League, a political-action organization. The NSL condemned fascism and racism and advocated civil

---

Elizabeth Kanouse is a homemaker who resides in Los Angeles.

I Was an Agnostic Unitarian / 61

liberties. Concerned with social and economic issues, the league generally worked for socialism. It was also antiwar, though I soon learned it was not against "imperialist" wars. Attracted by those sentiments, I joined the league. After several months I was elected chairman.

One day my new friends and I decided to drive to the San Pedro Harbor, where a longshoremen's strike was going on. We squeezed into a dilapidated truck and chugged off, singing lustily.

When we arrived at the dock, my comrades began to slash the tires of cars belonging to the strike breakers. They shouted obscenities and scuffled with the scabs. They resisted the police, and two were jailed briefly. On the ride home they boasted of their exploits. Though I was sympathetic with the strikers, as a law-respecting citizen I deplored my comrades' tactics.

I began to suspect that the NSL was a Communist front. Though the rank and file members were probably not Communists, I was disturbed by the radical ideas of the leaders and organizers I met after I became chairman. Their sympathies were with the Soviet Union, not the United States.

After being a member of the league for about six months, I submitted my resignation. No one tried to change my mind.

Next I tried meditation. There was a diminutive chapel on campus where one could reflect between classes. The charm of this structure with stained-glass windows and an open Bible soothed my unsettled thoughts. Here in solitude the seeker could contemplate God, if there was one, and imagine what He was like.

To my mind He was the infinite spirit of love, goodness, and truth, and I yearned for the mystical rapture of union with Him. But this God was distant, impersonal, unobtainable. As for Jesus, to me He was a great religious leader, nothing more.

I acquired these views as naturally as I had my political ideology. My parents were Unitarians, who believed in God but did not subscribe to the trinitarian doctrine of the deity of Jesus and the Holy Spirit, along with the Father. During my high school years, I attended a Unitarian youth group. We discussed such questions as, "Are Unitarians Christians?"

But my father loved the Bible and insisted on my memorizing some of the great passages: the Shepherd Psalm, the Lord's Prayer, the love chapter of 1 Corinthians, and the faith chapter of Hebrews. These had become a part of me.

As an English major in college I was intrigued by a course called "The Bible as Literature" which stimulated in me a desire to read the Bible for its meaning. But I was too busy with my other studies to concentrate on it.

During the summer following my graduate year, I began my quest, by reading the New Testament. I was determined to read with an open mind. I wanted to learn more about Jesus. Beginning with the first three Gospels, I marked the margins with questions on passages difficult for me to understand or accept.

My stumbling block was the miracles. Jesus said, "None of you will ever believe unless you see miracles and wonders" (John 4:48, TEV). But I could not believe *because* of the wonders.

All my training in logic and debate impelled me to shudder in disbelief—from the miraculous birth of Jesus to His empty tomb; from His exorcising of a demon-possessed man to His raising Jairus' daughter from the sleep of death; from His calming of the storm to His walking on the sea. I regarded these as legends that defied the laws of nature.

While I was a house guest of my friend Kay, I was alone briefly and picked up a book from the coffee table. In it were the answers to my questions, and I began to devour its pages. Having discovered this treasure, I grasped every opportunity to read E. Stanley Jones' *Victorious Living* (Abingdon).

Finally Kay declared in exasperation, "Look, Elizabeth, you came to visit me! I'll loan you the book, and when you get home you can read to your heart's content."

I did exactly that. It was as though the author had written it with me in mind. The author's logic impressed me as he led me step-by-step from doubt to belief. His concern both for individual salvation and suffering humanity attracted me. His portrayal of Jesus captivated me. Dr. Jones began where I stood when he wrote:

"It would be well if, in our quest for victorious living, we could all begin with God . . . . But, alas, many of us cannot begin there. For God is the vague, the unreal . . . . We find ourselves questioning life itself. Has life any meaning? The issues of life are before me. I must vote for or against a view of life which has worth, purpose, goal . . . . I vote for life.

"You must make your choice: either you must dismiss Christ entirely from life and forget Him . . . or you must make a complete surrender of every withheld area into the control of Christ."

The issue was now before me. The choice was mine to make. Even the failure to decide would be in itself a choice—against Jesus. Yet doubt concerning His identity persisted. I needed to know His credentials.

I turned again to the New Testament and read the Gospel of John. The evidence that Jesus believed Himself to be the Son of God was overwhelming. He said: "I am the Bread of Life (John 6:48, TEV), the Light of the World (8:12), the Gate for the Sheep (10:7), the Good Shepherd (10:11), the Son of God (6:40), the resurrection and life (11:25), the way, the truth, and the life (14:6), and the real vine" (15:1). He also said, "Before Abraham was born I Am" (8:58).

When Pilate asked, "So You are a king?" Jesus answered, "You say that I am a king. For this I have been born and for this I have come into the world to bear to the truth" (John 18:37). After the Resurrection when Thomas exclaimed, "My Lord and my God!" Jesus said to him, "Do you believe because you see Me? How happy are those who believe without seeing Me!" (20:28-29)

Though Jesus believed in His own divinity, my question remained: Was He the unique Son of God?

First, C.S. Lewis in *Mere Christianity,* and later, Josh McDowell in *More than a Carpenter,* reasoned that Jesus was either a liar, a lunatic, or Lord. In view of His life and teachings, He could not have been a liar. In view of His wisdom and stability, He could not have been a lunatic. The other alternative was that Jesus is who He claimed to be: Christ, the Son of God.

I struggled with this dilemma, but by the time I read to the end of John's Gospel, I was convinced that Jesus is who He said He is. So the miracles seemed but the natural issue of His divine nature. I acknowledged Jesus and promised to follow Him. I went to a community church, and by faith I came to know Him as my Saviour who shed His blood for my sins, and as the indwelling Christ who helps me with my tasks and trials.

Reflecting on my past, I am convinced that while I was seeking God, He was first seeking me. He put the hunger and thirst in my heart and these could not be satisfied apart from Him. His hand led me to a college course in the Gospels, which opened my mind to who He is.

Yet there was no immediate change in my character. My

decision was a matter of the intellect, a conscious choice, but my instincts needed to be brought into line. The Holy Spirit took over, cleansing and directing my life.

But because I withheld some areas, yielding my will to God was a long process. The way has not always been easy, nor victorious. Yet self-centeredness has gradually given way to Christ-centeredness and new life.

Now I have found my cause. Christ's purpose is my purpose. No political-economic system can solve national and worldwide problems until people first put their trust in God. The kingdom of God is the hope of the world; so with zeal I serve and pray, "Thy kingdom come!"

Jesus said that the kingdom of God is within. This is where it begins—in each believer's heart. He harnesses my talent and skills for His church, our home, and the community. He gives me strength and health. He forgives my flaws. I find love, joy, and peace from God, who is my Father; from Jesus, who is my constant companion; and from the Holy Spirit, who is transforming me into the image of Christ.

Though I am but an unfinished likeness of my Lord, I understand what Paul meant when he said: "We Christians actually do have within us a portion of the very thoughts and mind of Christ" (1 Corinthians 2:16, LB).

Darkness vs. Light

Unitarianism Says:

"I am willing to call myself a Christian only if in the next breath I am permitted to say in varying degrees I am also a Jew, a Hindu, and Moslem, a Buddhist, a Stoic, and an admirer of Akhenaton, Zoroaster, Confucius, Loa-Tse, and Socrates." (Jack Mendelsohn, *Why I Am A Unitarian*)

"What Unitarians and many liberals in other churches reject is the Calvinistic doctrine of the Fall of Man and the Depravity of Human Nature. We believe in the age-long Rise of Man, the dignity and divinity of human nature." (Bishop Barnes, *Indianapolis Unitarian Bulletin,* 1928)

"The doctrine of revelation of the absolute and indisputable authority of the Bible is alien to Unitarian faith and teaching." (Carl Chorowsky, *Look* magazine, March 8, 1955)

"Christ was sent to earth as a great moral teacher rather than as a mediator." (William Channing, *Who Was Who in Church History*)

The Bible Says:

"You shall have no other gods before Me." / "Do not go after other gods to serve them and to worship them." / "Turn to Me, and be saved, all the ends of the earth; for I am God, and there is no other." (Jehovah, *Exodus* 20:3; *Jeremiah* 25:6; *Isaiah* 45:22)

"Thus says the Lord, 'Cursed is the man who trusts in mankind and makes flesh his strength, and whose heart turns away from the Lord.'" / "Blessed is the man who trusts in the Lord." Prophet Jeremiah, *Jeremiah* 17:5, 7)

"All Scripture is inspired by God and profitable for teaching, for reproof, for correction, for training in righteousness." (Apostle Paul, *2 Timothy* 3:16)/"Until heaven and earth pass away, not the smallest letter or stroke shall pass away from the Law." (Jesus, *Matthew* 5:18)

"The Son of Man has come to seek and to save that which was lost." (Jesus, *Luke* 19:10) / "There is one God, and one mediator also between God and men, the man Christ Jesus, who gave Himself as a ransom for all." (Apostle Paul, *1 Timothy* 2:5-6)

8
Unity Almost Splintered My Faith

by Faye Myers

My eyes were closed and I was relaxed, but I didn't feel as if I was meditating. The minister was still chanting: "God is power, God is unity. . . ." Maybe if I concentrated more—I wanted that peace the minister talked about.

I'd recently moved to Memphis, Tennessee and it seemed that peace was far from me. There is no peace for the "different" people in this world. Coming from a small town in North Carolina and from a Christian Reformed background, I saw my first day on the campus how different I was from the typical Memphis State University student. Every person I met asked if I "got high" and as weeks passed any guys who took me for a Coke or on a date asked why I didn't go to bed with them. Dordt College, where I'd transferred from, seemed far away in lifestyle as well as in miles.

I had left Dordt in Sioux Center, Iowa after two years to concentrate on magazine journalism, and Tennessee was the option closest to home. During the first few weeks I felt it was the worst choice I'd ever made. But then Jessica, a friend from the dorm, introduced me to her church and religion, and at the time it seemed to be the "logical" escape I was looking for.

Faye Myers is a senior at Memphis State University and resides in Pantego, North Carolina.

Unity Almost Splintered My Faith / 67

The first time I attended a Unity service with Jessica, we drove up to a houselike building, and as we entered we were overwhelmed by hugs and hellos from the rest of the congregation. The minister warmly asked my name, while holding onto my hand, and then welcomed me with a huge hug. "Faye, we love you here. Come in, come in," he said. I followed Jessica's swinging blond hair to a seat.

"You wanted to know why my mother and I came to this church," she said as we sat. "Mother didn't like other churches condemning each other. If a Catholic and Baptist both believe in God, why shouldn't they both be right? Some people here believe in reincarnation or evolution, but no one condemns anyone for what he believes or does. Whatever you feel is right, you can do."

Jessica's lifestyle showed this, I thought. She giggled. "The last church party I went to I was too drunk to get home."

After a few songs, someone dimmed the lights and the leader told us to get into a comfortable position. "We are going to elevate our minds and commune with God," the minister said. He chanted about unity and power and awakening the god within us. But somehow it didn't work for me. I could never lose awareness of things and people around me as the minister said we would.

I noticed too in his sermon that day, or "lecture" as Jessie called it, that he referred to Thoreau and Socrates as much as he did to the Bible and Christ. "They were wise men too," Jessica explained. It made sense to the philosophy-minded side of me.

Weeks passed and I attended regularly. In the meantime, I met Roberta and Sharon, two girls from The Navigators, a Christian fellowship group on campus. They were trying to start a Bible study in the dorm. I agreed to hold it in my room the following Monday night. But Monday nights I also had a class with Jessie, and afterward she always wanted to go for a drink. We did, and as a result I wasn't in a condition that night to concentrate on the lesson, which bothered me because it was about the scope of God's salvation, something I wanted to discuss.

Jessie's free lifestyle was becoming more and more my own. And the loving, hugging congregation members were becoming my family and friends. Still, Roberta and Sharon attracted me with their straight biblical approach that was so close to my Christian Reformed upbringing. I continued with the Bible studies.

After one Sunday's lecture I began to seriously wonder about

Unity's beliefs. The speaker was explaining how optimistic thinking could accomplish anything. "Our good friend Bernard (a man in the congregation stood up) told me last week that he and his wife had not sold one pair of shoes since their store opened three months ago. Then he applied Unity's teachings on optimistic thinking and has sold 32 pairs this week alone!" The congregation applauded.

After the lecture the minister made his usual announcements, including one on seminars held in Unity Village, Missouri. I could recall television ads about Unity's teachings on optimism and love. I wondered about this optimistic thinking, about finding God in my mind when meditating, and other Unity teachings. I asked Jessica on our way out. She stopped in the entry and picked up a few pamphlets.

When I got to my dorm room, I paged through them several times. The church I had attended and almost become a part of didn't believe Christ was God. Christ was only a perfect man such as we all could become. And the Unity religion didn't believe in sin. Sin was only pessimistic thoughts learned through traditions. Begun by a doctor, Unity became an organized religion several decades ago, and is now spread nationwide. Its headquarters are in Unity Village, Missouri.

Meanwhile, Roberta and Sharon had invited me to a weekend retreat of The Navigators. During the trip to the retreat center, Roberta and I discussed Unity. "You've got to have your basis in the Bible," Roberta said, and then she gave me a verse to memorize: "Two are better than one, because they have a good return for their labor. For if either of them falls, the one will lift up his companion. But woe to the one who falls when there is not another to lift him up" (Ecclesiastes 4:9-10). Besides getting me into the Word, the verse helped me see I was falling with Jessie and needed Christian companions like Roberta and Sharon.

That weekend we concentrated on Bible study. I felt much closer to God, letting Him speak directly to me through His Word, rather than through Thoreau or Socrates. I drifted away from Jessica and Unity and began attending church with Navigator friends.

The Lord had proved to me how much I needed His Word and Christian companions, rather than the false sense of security and the hugs of my Unity family and friends.

Darkness vs. Light

Unity Says:

"Christ is the only begotten Son of God, the one complete idea of perfect man and divine Mind. This Christ or perfect-man idea existing eternally in divine Mind is the true, spiritual, higher-self of every individual." (*Metaphysical Bible Dictionary,* Unity School of Christianity)

"Being 'born again' or 'born from above' is not a miraculous change that takes place in man; it is the establishment of that which has always existed as the perfect-man idea of divine Mind." (Charles Fillmore, *Christian Healing*)

"These theories of the sin offering of Jesus are conceived with the personal God idea. They carry out the pagan concept of a big god who becomes very angry with his disobedient children and can be mollified only with a human sacrifice." (Charles and Cora Fillmore, *Teach Us to Pray*)

"In man a wonderful being is in process of creation. This being is spiritual man, who will be equal with God, when he overcomes or handles with wisdom and power, the faculties of the body." (Charles Fillmore, *Twelve Powers of Man*)

The Bible Says:

"God highly exalted Him, and bestowed on Him the name which is above every name, that at the name of Jesus every knee should bow ... and that every tongue should confess that Jesus Christ is Lord." (Apostle Paul, *Philippians* 2:9-11)

"Unless one is born again, he cannot see the kingdom of God." (Jesus, *John* 3:3) / "You have been born again not of seed which is perishable but ... through the living and abiding Word of God." (Apostle Peter, *1 Peter* 1:23)

"God demonstrates His own love toward us, in that while we were yet sinners, Christ died for us." (Apostle Paul, *Romans* 5:8) / "If we walk in the light as He Himself is in the light ... the blood of Jesus His Son cleanses us from all sin." (Apostle John, *1 John* 1:7)

"You are just a vapor that appears for a little while and then vanishes away." (Apostle James, *James* 4:14) / "All souls are Mine. ... The soul who sins will die." / "I have no pleasure in the death of anyone who dies," declares the Lord God. "Therefore, repent and live." (Jehovah, *Ezekiel* 18:4, 32)

"Pain, sickness, poverty, old age, and death are not real, and they have no power over me. There is nothing in all the universe for me to fear." (H. Emily Cady, *Lessons In Truth*)

"Unity teaches that the eternal life taught and demonstrated by Jesus is not gained by dying, but by purifying the body until it becomes the undying habitation of the soul." (Charles Fillmore, *Unity* magazine, July 1922)

"We believe that the dissolution of spirit, soul, and body caused by death is annulled by rebirth of the same spirit and soul in another body here on earth. We believe the repeated incarnations of man to be a merciful provision of our loving Father to the end that all may have opportunity to obtain immortality through regeneration as did Jesus." *(Unity Statement of Faith, Article 22)*

"Do not fear those who kill the body, but are unable to kill the soul; but rather fear Him who is able to destroy both body and soul in hell." (Jesus, *Matthew* 10:28)

"Our citizenship is in heaven, from which also we eagerly wait for a Saviour, the Lord Jesus Christ, who will transform the body of our humble state into conformity with the body of His glory." (Apostle Paul, *Philippians* 3:20-21)

"When the Son of Man comes in His glory . . . then He will sit on His glorious throne." / "Then the King will say to those on His right, 'Come, you who are blessed of My Father; inherit the kingdom prepared for you.'" / "Then He will also say to those on His left, 'Depart from Me, accursed ones, into the eternal fire which has been prepared for the devil and his angels." (Jesus, *Matthew* 25:31, 34, 41)

9
I Talked with Spirits
by Victor Ernest

I could hardly wait for the next séance so I could talk with my departed sister . . . six more days seemed like an eternity.

I had no doubt that Iris would be present, though we had failed on the first attempt. I had talked with the spirit world many times in my 21 years. I had listened to the spirits give lectures, sermons, exhortations, and counsel to the group assembled at our home séances. But I had never tried to talk with a dead person.

My family, especially my mother's relatives, had been involved with spiritualism for several generations. They came to the United States from Holland before the Spanish-American War. My father was a very religious man. He often remarked that he would become a spiritualist if any of his five children were to die.

Soon after my seven-year-old sister, Iris, died, a family from nearby Bemidji, Minnesota told us they had contacted the spirit of my dead sister and that she was eager to talk with us. The whole family was excited, and we agreed to be in Bemidji at the appointed time for the séance.

There were perhaps 10 people gathered for the séance. We sat

The Rev. Victor Ernest heads Vital Christian Concerns, a counseling ministry, and travels widely for speaking engagements. His address is 434 Taylor Street, Anoka, MN 55303.

quietly and expectantly. The medium, a man, sat at one end of our semicircle of chairs and led us in singing hymns and in prayer.

It didn't seem strange to us to open the séance by saying the Lord's Prayer. We even ended "in the name of the Father, Son, and Holy Spirit." A prayer for a séance went like this:

"Eternal God and Father of Lights, we gather as thy expectant children. We are eager to communicate with the spirit world and the spirits of our departed friends and loved ones. We pray that you would look favorably upon us. Bless us this night with communications from our friends in the spirit world. In the name of the great Father of Lights. Amen."

Then we sang familiar church hymns such as "Face to Face," "In the Garden," "Beautiful Isle of Somewhere," and "Nearer My God to Thee."

While we were singing, the medium slumped into unconsciousness, and before long a strange voice spoke through the medium's lips; it was the control spirit.

"Good evening, my children. There are many of the departed here, and all are eager to speak with you. The spirit world welcomes you to another opportunity to contact your departed loved ones."

We listened eagerly to the spirit as the medium sat limply, eyes closed, in his chair. The spirit said that a family was present whose departed loved one wanted very much to speak with them, but since she had been in the spirit world so short a time, she was still adjusting to her new spiritual dimension and would have to communicate the following week. That was a terrible disappointment, and the whole family could hardly wait until the next séance when we could contact our beloved sister.

At the second meeting we encountered another phase of spiritualism, the trumpet séance (sometimes called a "séance of vocal revelation"). A metal trumpet, made of aluminum or sheet metal, stood upright in a damp saucer on a table in the middle of the room. When the medium entered his trance, the trumpet rose slowly from the table and dipped into a horizontal position. Eerily, it began spinning with a soft whir and moved around the room, stopping at intervals in midair.

I sat rigid in amazement. I saw the floating trumpet, but I could not believe it. The residents of the home seemed to accept the experience as very common.

The trumpet went first to my mother and then to other members of our family. And we heard a voice, supposedly my departed sister's, but at first we could not distinguish the words.

Then the trumpet came to me. My first reaction was to grab it, and I snatched at the mouthpiece, but it darted away with amazing swiftness. I tried again, but it moved faster than I did. The trumpet finally settled directly in front of me, just out of my reach.

Then the control spirit launched into a lecture about my unbelief, speaking through the unconscious medium. He said I must conduct myself in dignity and orderliness if I were to benefit from the meeting. As my emotions subsided, the trumpet hovered closer and closer to me until it was near my ear, its tip stroking my hair in the way my sister used to comb it.

A voice flowed from the trumpet saying, "I love you; I love you." It was supposed to be my sister's voice, but it did not sound like her to me. Everyone else accepted it as Iris' voice, but I was disappointed; it was not Iris. That was the first of many occasions when she supposedly spoke to the family, but I was never convinced.

At later séances an older sister and I were told we could become gifted spirit mediums. By following the instructions of the spirit voice in the séance of passivity, we would in time be able to contact the spirits in our own home.

This sister and I began to practice the séance of passivity for five, six, then seven minutes each evening, adding one minute each time. During these periods we tried to blot out every conscious thought from our minds. Eventually we could sit for 15- and 20-minute-periods without being distracted by a single conscious thought.

In one of the longer periods, the phenomenon we had been waiting for finally took place. I witnessed the spirit taking control of my sister as she lost consciousness and a voice completely foreign to her soft contralto boomed out:

"My child, be not afraid. You have done well. Greater things than these you will do if you only believe. Continue in this way, and the marvels of the spirit world will be revealed to you."

With that, the spirit departed and my sister regained consciousness. She asked what had happened, and I told her the words of the spirit. She was thrilled! She had arrived at a coveted place of spiritual development, and from that time on we held séances in our home for other people, with my sister as the gifted medium.

Some people say this is all a hoax, that spirits do not talk with human beings and that floating objects are mere trickery. I would agree that a great many of the eerie demonstrations we hear about are clever illusions, but I believe on the basis of personal experience and the plain words of Scripture that spirits of the invisible world do communicate with humanity and do wield supernatural power in our visible world. However, the ominous truth is that these spirits are not from God but are fallen angels controlled by Satan. Their unholy mission is to lead human beings—by refined or gross means—away from dependence on God, their Creator, and they are active in spiritualist churches, séances, psychic phenomena, witchcraft, and idol worship. Individuals and nations who reject God, no matter how educated and prosperous they are, fall prey to the god, Satan.

Spiritualism makes headlines and feature stories in the guise of horoscopes, ominous predictions, and bizarre cults, but its basic activity is the séance where many people can be influenced. And the key that opens the séance is the trance.

In the séance, the "alleged supernatural agency" is the control spirit who takes possession of the medium. This spirit is not the same as the familiar spirit.

In spiritualist teaching, the familiar spirit is a spirit from God who is with us from birth and on into eternity. We may have many familiar spirits during a lifetime as we progress in moral goodness. Spirits are assigned to individuals and come to know them better than they know themselves.

Spiritualists believe in an evolutionary process of spiritual development. Individuals departing from this life are said to migrate to the spirit world and develop there with the help of other spirits. Theoretically, a person could advance in the spirit world to the level of God Himself. However, spiritualists believe that God also is evolving to higher and higher planes. Therefore, the best the spirit of the departed can do is reach a plane where God once was.

Prophecy plays a large part in a spiritualist séance. At one séance I participated in, where the medium was a member of my family, World War II was prophesied and the nations that would be engulfed in this gigantic conflict were named. I also remember the control spirit saying, "At the end of World War II there will be no end of war upon the face of the earth until the kingdom of peace is come."

Spiritualists believe that Jesus is the master medium of all mediums. To them, God is a universal force, not a person. Spiritualists maintain that heaven is nothing more than the series of planes where the spirit evolves. They teach there is no such place as hell—unless that would describe the existence of an earthbound spirit. Yet, significantly—and ominously for all people who choose to live in sin rather than in God's will—spiritualists recognize the existence of the devil, the source of all evil.

Some spiritualist teaching is similar to the beliefs of Buddhism, Zoroastrianism, Theosophy, and other religions. And spiritualism's rosy prospect of becoming gods over individual realms is matched by the Mormons (Church of Jesus Christ of Latter-Day Saints).

My mother was not trained in the Bible, but she loved what she knew of God's Word. Early in my life she had taught me about God's existence, creation, and power. I began to wonder what the Bible teaches, and I determined to buy one.

I began to read in Genesis. The story of the Creation was familiar to me, but before long I got bogged down in the genealogies. Thinking that the Bible was like any other book, I decided to turn to the end to see how it all turned out.

I got mired down again, this time in the symbolism of the Revelation. A little discouraged, I almost set my Bible to one side. However, I was reluctant to let my investment lie idle.

The first book I read in its entirety was the First Epistle of John. When I got to the fourth chapter, I read with amazement: "Beloved, believe not every spirit, but try the spirits" (v. 1, KJV).

This was just what I wanted. This must mean there were good spirits and bad spirits. I read on:

". . . whether they are of God: because many false prophets are gone out into the world. Hereby know ye the Spirit of God: every spirit that confesseth that Jesus Christ is come in the flesh is of God; and every spirit that confesseth not that Jesus Christ is come in the flesh is not of God; and this is that spirit of antichrist, whereof ye have heard that it should come; and even now already is it in the world" (1 John 4:1-3, KJV).

I decided at the next séance I attended I would "try the spirits," though I didn't know how to go about it.

76 / Escape from Darkness

I was amazed when the control spirit at the next meeting announced it would be a question-and-answer séance, and even specified that the questions were to be of a spiritual nature. This had never happened in any séance I attended.

I directed my first question to the control spirit in fear and trembling, as the floating trumpet stood before me. I asked if he believed that Jesus was the Son of God.

The control spirit answered smoothly, "Of course, my child; Jesus is the Son of God. Only believe as the Bible says."

I had never heard a spirit affirm this. In other séances I had often heard that Jesus was a great medium or a Judean reformer, and that now He was an advanced spirit on a higher plane.

Before long, the trumpet came back to me, and I had to ask a second question. Since they allowed only three questions each, I was anxious to make mine count. This time I falteringly asked, "O thou great and infinite spirit, do you believe that Jesus is the Saviour of the world?"

Almost before my words were uttered, the answer came: "My child, why do you doubt? Why do you not believe? You have been this long with us; why do you continue to doubt?" Then the spirit began to quote Scripture about believing.

I don't remember the verses, but they sounded authentic to me; the spirit quoted Scripture readily, if not accurately.

When the trumpet returned for my third and last question, I reviewed what the spirit had said. "O spirit, you believe that Jesus is the Son of God, that He is the Saviour of the world—do you believe that Jesus died on the cross and shed His blood for the remission of sin?"

The medium, in a deep trance, was catapulted off his chair. He fell in the middle of the living room floor and lay groaning as if in deep pain. The turbulent sounds suggested spirits in a carnival of confusion.

We all rushed forward to help him. The control spirit had prepared us with instructions on how to revive a person in such an emergency, and we massaged the pulse areas until he revived.

I never went to another séance. I had tested the spirits and found they were not of God. What I had thought to be a great power of God, the utopia of religious experience, had burst like a bubble. I realized that I had been in contact with the counterfeit of what God has to offer—and I wanted His reality. From that time I began to search God's Word to find the truth.

In my early study of the Bible, I had no difficulty believing in God, but I soon saw that to believe in God was not enough. Jesus had said, "Believe also in Me" (John 14:1). To believe in God as Creator was one thing; to believe in Jesus as Saviour was another, especially when He had to be my personal Saviour.

As I read the Bible, haphazardly turning here and there, I came upon a marvelous passage: "In hope of eternal life, which God, who cannot lie, promised us before the world began . . ." (Titus 1:2, KJV). What a joy to realize that God, in the very nature of His being, is a person who cannot lie, who is perfect holiness.

I found Romans 3:23, "For all have sinned and come short of the glory of God" (KJV). Connecting this with Romans 6:23, "For the wages of sin is death; but the gift of God is eternal life through Jesus Christ our Lord" (KJV), I thought about how cheaply I was "working" as far as my life was concerned. My wage, as a sinner, was death! I decided to go on strike against my employer.

I understood that God in His love wanted to give me eternal life and that I was in need of that gift. I also knew that I couldn't buy it, and I couldn't earn it.

I discovered in the Gospel of John how I could receive God's gift: "But as many as received Him [Christ], to them gave He power to become the sons of God, even to them that believe on His name" (1:12, KJV).

How did I go about receiving Him? How does one receive anything? Ask and then accept what is offered. There was no thought in my mind that God would turn me down, because I knew that He had gone to the cross to save me. Having already gone to such lengths for me, He would not refuse me now. There my reasoning ended, and my faith began. In faith I realized that if I did my part, God would certainly do His.

I don't know how long I talked with God that October night, but it was a long time. Finally, a great peace came into my heart, and I thanked the Lord that He had heard me, received me, and saved me. Since then I thank Him many times daily that He has kept me for Himself.

"Verily, verily, I say unto you, he that heareth My Word, and believeth on Him that sent Me, hath everlasting life, and shall not come into condemnation; but is passed from death unto life" (John 5:24, KJV). I thank the Lord for this promise from the God who cannot lie. I passed from the family of the lost into the family of the saved, from Satan's family into God's family!

* * *

Here is a summary of the main facts about spiritualism in relation to the Christian faith of the Bible:

(1) Because a phenomenon is spiritual does not necessarily mean it is an act of God.

(2) The true character of spirits can be exposed by their rejection of Jesus Christ as God the Son who died to atone for mankind's sin.

(3) A familiar spirit in the service of Satan knows human beings so well that he can disguise himself as those people. (The late James A. Pike went to several mediums who told him they had contacted his dead son, Jim, Jr., and that father and son could communicate in a séance. Pike supposedly did so on a number of occasions, as he describes in his book *The Other Side*. Actually, Pike talked with a spirit who was familiar with his son. This spirit impersonated his son so well and favorably that Pike overcame his remorse about his son's suicide, and looked forward to rejoining his son.)

(4) There are different kinds of spirits (see Mark 9:29); some are sensual and lewd, and others appear ethical.

(5) Demons are wandering spirits belonging to the legions of Satan, a class of beings distinct from angels—some are on earth seeking embodiment in human beings and animals, others already are imprisoned in the bottomless abyss.

(6) God has forbidden humans to try to communicate with the departed dead; such attempts result in communication with deceitful spirits known as "familiar" spirits.

(7) Satan wins followers by psychic and supernatural phenomena that approximate the power of God.

(8) Satan is a created being who presently exercises authority over his domain, the earth realm, but he can do only what God allows him to do, and eventually he will be deprived of all power.

(9) Satan attacks at the Christian's vulnerable points, often where the Christian thinks he is strong and secure—only vigilance and spiritual armor keep the Christian victorious.

(10) Guardian angels protect the Christian from demonic assaults that God will not permit. The true Christian is securely on the winner's side!

Darkness vs. Light

Spiritualism Says:

"There is only one universe. There is no other 'heaven.' . . . It is only that you cannot see me. . . . My world is your world *plus*." (Bette White, *The Betty Book,* by Stewart Edward White)

"One can see no justice in a vicarious sacrifice, nor in the God who could be placated by such means." (A. Conan Doyle, *The New Revelation*)

"We must reject the conception of fallen creatures. By the Fall we understand the descent of spirit to matter." (G.G. Andre, *The True Light*)

"We affirm that the doorway to reformation is never closed against any human soul, here or hereafter." (*Declaration of Principles,* National Spiritualist Association)

"High above all these is the greatest spirit of whom they [the spirits] have cognizance—not God, since God is so infinite that he is not within their ken—but one who is nearer God and to that extent represents God. This is the Christ Spirit." (A. Conan Doyle, *The New Revelation*)

The Bible Says:

"Some will fall away from the faith, paying attention to deceitful spirits." (Apostle Paul, *1 Timothy* 4:1) / "Do not turn to mediums or spiritists . . . to be defiled by them." (Moses, *Leviticus* 19:31)

"The word of the Cross is to those who are perishing foolishness, but to us who are being saved it is the power of God. For it is written, 'I will destroy the wisdom of the wise.'" (Apostle Paul, *1 Corinthians* 1:18-19)

"Through one man sin entered into the world, and death through sin, and so death spread to all men, because all sinned." (Apostle Paul, *Romans* 5:12)

"No immoral or impure person or covetous man, who is an idolater, has an inheritance in the kingdom of Christ and God . . . because of these things the wrath of God comes upon the sons of disobedience." (Apostle Paul, *Ephesians* 5:5-6)

"Behold, the tabernacle of God is among men, and He shall dwell among them, and they shall be His people, and God Himself shall be among them, and He shall wipe away every tear from their eyes; and there shall no longer be any death." (God speaking to the Apostle John, *Revelation* 21:3-4)

10
The Moonies Almost Got Me

Anonymous

I had promised to meet someone in the downtown area of San Francisco, and I was lost. While I was standing, considering what to do, Sharon and Mary Anne—all bright eyes and smiles—approached me. I didn't know it, but I was an obvious candidate. My backpack signaled my availability and a vacationer's free time.

I had come from New York City hoping to meet new friends and experience life away from city hassles and personal frustrations. Externally, my life in New York had seemed to be going well. I had my own apartment in Manhattan and had started working in a quaint restaurant in Greenwich Village. Yet I was dissatisfied and unhappy. I longed for dependable Christian friends. When the restaurant closed for renovations, I gathered my savings and bought a ticket to San Francisco.

Sharon and Mary Anne invited me to their communal home for dinner. They seemed "normal," the name of their commune was the Creative Community Project, and a home-cooked meal sounded good to a backpacker.

They made me feel at home as soon as I entered the Washington Street house. I helped prepare the meal with the other guests. "I thought you guys were Moonies," I said jokingly. They denied this and laughed with me. Before and after the meal, we sang some familiar Christian songs and prayed to God. I concluded that I had found a Christian commune. We were encouraged to tell about our lives and to share our experiences with the open, sincere "family" members of this community.

After dinner there was a program and a leader asked everyone to sing or recite. I sang, arm-in-arm with three people I had met only an hour before. A lecture followed about three blind, wise men who encountered an elephant. They each touched a different part, and, because of their partial point of view, they each thought the elephant was something else. This story was told to illustrate the partial viewpoints of all men and the need to unify these viewpoints to reach the truth.

A slide presentation followed, showing a beautiful farm in Booneville, California where their ideas about changing society and living together with no sex and no drugs were to be discussed. They invited me to attend a three-day seminar, but at first I was skeptical and asked some questions. It sounded too good. Reassuringly, they said that I could leave any time I wanted. A $20 fee relieved my suspicion of "something for nothing." I had no definite plans, and this stay in the country was cheaper than a hotel and seemed safer than hitchhiking. They loaned me a coat for the cooler weather, and I persuaded Mitch, another new arrival that evening, to go. I felt warm, wanted, and safe. Little did I know that my openness, lack of skepticism, and free time were handles that would hold me with them.

At the farm, the schedule of the day was intense, structured, and entirely group-centered. From the very early "jumping it," when we bolted out of our sleeping bags with joyful songs, we were involved in activities and required to give 100 percent of ourselves. Negativity or judgment of any sort was banned. We were to remain open to the teachings from the three or four lengthy lectures each day. Discussions of our feelings took place regularly throughout the day. The Bible was read each day and used to reassure me that the ideas were from God, yet no Bibles were available for us. Time was packed to the minute with group activities from 7 A.M. to 11 P.M. There was no time to criticize the ideas I heard.

Sometimes after lunch we played dodge ball. Two teams tried to hit the opponents out, shouting slogans of "Love Conquers All" or "Fight with Love." Once you were out, you cheered the team slogan at the top of your lungs. I remember wanting to be alone, so

I didn't cheer. A "sister" warned me against being negative and said that everyone was needed to support their team. I joined reluctantly.

After the three-day retreat, the leaders invited us to stay and learn more. I felt confused, but I was discovering something new, and I had begun to feel close to the people. The talk of God and the Bible made me think that God was behind the group. It was easier to stay than to decide to leave.

After about a week, the group moved to Bambiland, a camp isolated in the redwood forest near Mendocino. Different lecturers repeated the preliminary lecture series. The topics dealt with God, the Creation, causes of evil, building a new world with love, and the unified logic which would be the basis for later "divine principle" lectures.

The preliminary lectures were easily acceptable. Only after a week and a half did I find that the group was in any way associated with Sun Myung Moon. They still denied that they were with the Unification Church. When Noah, a respected lecturer, talked about the Rev. Moon's life (after two and a half weeks), I was neither surprised nor angry at being deceived—I was accepting as logical and correct ideas which I would have normally rejected. Though I never accepted the Rev. Moon as the "Messiah," the idea that Jesus' mission on earth failed because of His death seemed plausible and in accord with the Scripture as quoted by these teachers.

About once a week, accompanied by a member of the group and advised on what to say, I called home to reassure my parents. In spite of my assurances, they sensed a change and a vagueness in my voice. After the third week, I knew that the group was the Unification Church. I wanted to go home and explain it to my parents. I spoke to Noah about doing so. He thought I was not strong enough in the "principle" and suggested that I stay the biblical 40 days. I felt comfortable with a set time, and my heart was committed to the people of the group. I planned to stay.

During a lecture one Thursday afternoon, I received a note telling me to come to the back of the room. There, to my surprise, were my parents. We embraced with great joy. They seemed so out of place. It was as if they had entered my dream with a reality that didn't fit. Behind the smiles I saw their fear, their love. They told me of deceit used by the Creative Community Project to make it difficult for them to contact me. Despite the obstacles (which were many), God led my parents to me only an hour before the group was to change camp.

I was not able, at that point, to assess the disorientation of isolation, the manipulation of group pressure, the force of professed love, the removal of definitive choices or critical analysis, the magnetism of a new world that one could build, the imposition of guilt for lack of commitment, the ultimate control of thought and activity, and the justification of deceit. Only later did those things become clear.

For weeks after I went home with my parents, my mind was flooded with songs, ideas, and feelings about the group. Momentarily I would long to be back and was afraid of the seeming void that lay ahead. Today I am grateful to God who led my parents to me, to my family and friends who prayed for me and received me with unconditional joy and love, and to Christian college students who provided a needed substitute community and the opportunity to grow in my faith.

Not all are so fortunate. When I left, Mitch was still there. As our car drove away, Mary Anne sadly stared out the window. I bear no ill will to these dedicated, misguided young people, who have been systematically deprived of free choice. I condemn those leaders who have constructed this system for their own power. They live on the profits, while their victims strive vainly for an unreal vision and a false messiah.

Darkness vs. Light

Unification Church Says:

"Jesus was not the unique, only begotten Son of God who was preexistent with the Father before all created things. Jesus attained deity, as a man who fulfilled the purpose of creation, but can by no means be considered God Himself." (Young Oon Kim, *Divine Principle and Its Application,* Holy Spirit Association for Unification of World Christianity)

"Jesus did not come to die on the cross. The crucifixion was the result of the ignorance and disbelief of the Jewish people." (Sun Myung Moon, *Divine Principle*)

"Jesus failed in his christly mission. His death on the cross was not an essential part of God's plan for redeeming mankind." (Young Oon Kim, *Divine Principle and Its Application*)

"He [God] is living in me and I am in the incarnation of Him. I am in His place to work for Him until the last one of all humanity has been turned back to Him." (Sun Moon, *New Hope*)

The Bible Says:

"God, after He spoke long ago to the fathers in the prophets in many portions and in many ways, in these last days has spoken to us in His Son, whom He appointed heir of all things, through whom also He made the world. And He is the radiance of His glory and the exact representation of His nature, and upholds all things by the word of His power." (Hebrews 1:1-3)

"The Son of man did not come to be served, but to serve, and to give His life a ransom for many." / "I lay down My life that I may take it again." (Jesus, *Mark* 10:45; *John* 10:17)

"We have been sanctified through the offering of the body of Jesus Christ once for all." / "He, having offered one sacrifice for sins for all time, sat down at the right hand of God, waiting from that time onward until His enemies be made a footstool for His feet." (*Hebrews* 10:10, 12-13)

"No one comes to the Father but through Me." (Jesus, *John* 14:6) / "There is salvation in no one else; for there is no other name under heaven that has been given among men, by which we must be saved." (Evangelist Luke, *Acts* 4:12)

The Moonies Almost Got Me / 85

"When you become God's champion for world salvation, your own salvation is guaranteed." (Sun Moon, *New Hope*)

"The New Testament was a textbook given for the teaching of the truth to the people of 2,000 years ago ... today the truth must appear with higher standards ... we call this the New Truth." (Sun Moon, *Divine Principle*)

"By grace you have been saved, through faith, and that not of yourselves, it is the gift of God; not as a result of works, that no one should boast." (Apostle Paul, *Ephesians* 2:8-9)

"If any man is preaching to you a gospel contrary to that which we have preached to you, let him be accursed." (Apostle Paul, *Galatians* 1:9)

11
Maharishi, Meditation, and Me

*by Reuben B. Rubin
as told to Darlene Paterson*

As I entered the luxurious Washington, D.C. hotel, I wondered if this encounter would end my search for the things missing in my life—love, peace, and fulfillment. The clean white handkerchief I was told to bring was tucked in my pocket, and my wallet contained the required $75. I also carried the necessary flowers and fruit. I was ready for the initiation ceremony.

A shiver of excitement went through me as I sat in the waiting room. Surely this would be the life-changing experience I was searching for. I should have known something about the meaning of life. I was 23, had a master's degree in interpersonal communication from Ohio University, and taught communication courses at Howard University in Washington. Yet I didn't have the ability to apply the principles I was teaching to myself.

I tried studying psychology, which revealed my errant nature but didn't give an answer for it. I came to the conclusion that life's problems were of a deep, spiritual nature.

My modern-day Jewish parents had told me that the personal God I'd heard about at the synagogue probably didn't exist. "God

---

Reuben B. Rubin was ministering with Jews for Jesus on the West Coast when he wrote this article. Later he became associated with another ministry in Tennessee.
Darlene Paterson is a free-lance writer who lives in Arlington, Washington.

wouldn't allow such atrocities as Nazi Germany to happen if He cared about His chosen people," they reasoned.

I had always wondered what it meant to be Jewish. According to a Jewish tradition, a spark of the divine is in each of us. But I knew I was as sinful as anyone. So I looked elsewhere for the answer to my inner search—and didn't find what I was looking for. The whole world seemed in turmoil. Was there no answer to the racial tension, pollution, war, violence, and hate that prevailed in the world?

Then I heard about Transcendental Meditation. I attended three introductory lectures and was told that TM promises higher states of consciousness, greater physical well-being, and inner peace. This fit in with my humanistic background. I decided to try TM—and that decision led me to the hotel.

My mind snapped to attention as a young man, my "initiator," approached. He led me into a quiet, candle-lit room permeated with the sweet smell of incense. We knelt before a small altar on which a picture of the Maharishi Mahesh Yogi was sitting. The Maharishi, an Indian guru, brought TM to the Western world. Next to his picture was one of his departed leader, Guru Dev (Divine Master).

My initiator took my money and placed the flowers and fruit on the handkerchief in front of the pictures, offering them in homage to the gurus. Then he began chanting in Sanskrit the names of Hindu gods, invoking their power as he began a ceremonial ritual.

At the conclusion of the ceremony, my teacher looked at me and made a sound like "sh-ing." This was to be my mantra—the sound that would help me transcend into new levels of consciousness. He told me to repeat it over and over. The repetition had a hypnotic effect on me.

"Say it softer! Softer! Now say it in your mind," he whispered.

The moment I switched from voicing audible words to repeating the mantra in my mind, I experienced a sinking or descending sensation. A chill of fear went down my spine, immediately bringing me back to reality. My teacher told me to meditate a while longer, and he left. I sat and wondered if what I had experienced was real or just my imagination.

The next spring I met a girl who was also a meditator, and my involvement in TM deepened through her influence. I became a TM fanatic, and recommended it to all my friends as the answer to their problems. Not many listened, for they didn't see it solving mine. Actually, as a result of TM, I was losing my self-confidence. My mind was so messed up, I had to quit teaching.

I dedicated myself completely to TM, attending weekend residence courses and making plans to become a teacher of Transcendental Meditation. I spent a month on a beautiful California beach, enjoying delicious food and fellowship with 1,400 other seekers of truth. We studied from the ancient Hindu Vedic scriptures with the Maharishi himself. I experienced many supernatural "evidences" while meditating. At times I thought I heard someone calling my name. Often I felt as if someone were touching me. Convinced TM was the cure-all, I made plans to go to Spain for two months of study before becoming a teacher.

Shortly after, during a weekend residence course in TM, a strange thing happened. During one of my eight meditations for that day, I felt as if my soul left my body. When I came out of the trance, I was shaking with fright. I felt the need for a change of pace.

Finding a Gideon Bible in the hotel room where I was staying, I began to read. I'd never read the New Testament, and I was surprised to find it had a lot to say about the Jews. I flipped over to Revelation and read about the last days. I shook my head. *There aren't going to be any last days. TM is going to save the world.* I laid the Bible aside, but couldn't forget what I had read.

Not long after this, two fellows in my Coast Guard Reserve unit spoke to me about Jesus Christ. They told me that I could have peace and fulfillment by committing my life to Jesus, the Messiah. I attended a Rosh Hashanah (Jewish New Year) service put on by a Hebrew Christian group, and was attracted by an intangible source of joy in the lives of these Jewish believers.

Attending Bible studies with an organization called Jews for Jesus, I searched the Scriptures on my own. The more I studied the Bible, the more convinced I became that Jesus Christ fulfilled all the prophecies concerning the Messiah.

Finally, convinced that Jesus Christ was the Messiah, and feeling His love reaching out to me, I realized I had to choose between Jesus and Transcendental Meditation. I couldn't have both.

But I had invested hundreds of dollars and three years of my life in TM. Was I willing to give it up for Jesus?

Yes! I chose Jesus. I knew He was "the way, and the truth, and the life" (John 14:6) I had been searching for. I confessed my sins and turned my life over to Him. Jesus has given me true joy and peace which could never be matched by the counterfeit peace I'd received through practicing TM.

On July 4, 1975 I married Steffi, a beautiful Jewish Christian. She had been praying for my salvation. We became part of the Jews for Jesus ministry, speaking to many people about Christ.

Unlike the "promises" offered by Transcendental Meditation, the real God has provided *real* blessings in my life. My search has ended because I know the Truth—and the Truth is Jesus, the Messiah.

Darkness vs. Light

Transcendental Meditation Says:

"The Absolute is said to be almighty but not in the sense It is able to do everything. This is because being everything, It cannot do anything and cannot know anything. It is beyond doing and knowing." (Maharishi Mahesh Yogi, *Transcendental Meditation*)

"We do something here according to Vedic rites, particular specific chanting to produce an effect in some other world, draw the attention of those higher beings or gods living there." (Maharishi, *Transcendental Meditation*)

"We are all 100 percent Divine; consciously we do not know that we are Divine." (Maharishi, *Meditations of Maharishi*)

"It is a pity that Christ is talked of in terms of suffering. . . . Those who count upon the suffering [for salvation have] a wrong interpretation of the life of Christ and the message of Christ." (Maharishi, *Transcendental Meditation*)

"Death as such only causes a temporary pause in the process of evolution." (Maharishi, *On the Bhagavad-Gita*)

The Bible Says:

"We have received . . . the Spirit who is from God, that we might know the things freely given to us by God." / "But a natural man does not accept the things of the Spirit of God; for . . . he cannot understand them, because they are spiritually appraised." (Apostle Paul, *1 Corinthians* 2:12, 14)

"When you are praying, do not use meaningless repetition, as the Gentiles do, for they suppose that they will be heard for their many words . . . your Father knows what you need, before you ask Him." (Jesus, *Matthew* 6:7-8)

"Both Jews and Greeks are all under sin; as it is written, 'There is none righteous, not even one.'" (Apostle Paul, *Romans* 3:9-10)

"It is written, that the Christ should suffer and rise again from the dead the third day." (Jesus, *Luke* 24:46) / "And He Himself bore our sins in His body on the cross, that we might die to sin and live to righteousness; for by His wounds you were healed." (Apostle Peter, *1 Peter* 2:24)

"When a wicked man dieth, his expectation shall perish; and the hope of unjust men perisheth." (Solomon, *Proverbs* 11:7, KJV)

"Indifference is the weapon to be used against any negative situation in life." (Maharishi, *On The Bhagavad-Gita*)

"[TM] is the only way to salvation and success in life; there is no other way." (Maharishi, *On The Bhagavad-Gita*)

"Open your mouth, judge righteously, and defend the rights of the afflicted and needy." (Lemuel, *Proverbs* 31:9-10)

"There is a way which seems right to a man, but its end is the way of death." (Solomon, *Proverbs* 14:12) / "I am the way, and the truth, and the life; no one comes to the Father but through Me." (Jesus, *John* 14:6)

12
Hare Krishna Starved My Soul

*by Ed Senesi
as told to Eric Pement*

I first became interested in the Vedic scriptures and Eastern spirituality about the time I started experimenting with various kinds of hallucinogenic drugs. I know from personal experience that over 90 percent, maybe 99 percent of the people that I dealt with in ISKCON—The International Society for Krishna Consciousness—joined at a point when they were experimenting with LSD or other hallucinogenic drugs.

I chose ISKCON because of the commitment that I saw in the members: their withdrawal from the materialistic world, their total immersion into life, and a complete dedication to God. I hadn't seen that in the clergy, or in the Roman Catholic Church in which I'd been raised. I thought if God was to reveal Himself to anybody, He would reveal Himself to people who were totally dedicated to Him.

I guess the thing that turned me away from traditional Christianity, or Judeo-Christian theology, was a growing belief in reincarnation. I thought, "What kind of God would subject His

---

Ed Senesi, an honors graduate of Fairleigh Dickinson University, Rutherford, New Jersey, is active in speaking on the subject of cults and lives in Los Angeles.
Eric Pement is a writer for Cornerstone magazine.

beloved children to an eternity of suffering on the basis of mistakes they had committed in one lifetime?" To me, the punishment didn't fit the crime; if you were a murderer, an adulterer, or a thief in one lifetime, it didn't merit you an eternity of suffering with no chance of escape.

"If that's the God of Christianity, I don't want to have anything to do with Him," I reasoned, and started becoming attracted to the philosophy and theology of Eastern culture and the Hare Krishna movement. I became more convinced of the concepts of reincarnation and of karma—the theory of paying for one's failures in a subsequent life. I wasn't attracted to TM because I didn't want to learn a meditative technique that would only improve my materialistic life. I wanted to know God and I wanted to know Him completely.

To me, the Krishnas said essentially what I'd been taught as a Catholic, with the exception of reincarnation and karma. They believed in living a good life, a clean and pure life, dedicated to God. They didn't take drugs, or go to night clubs, or become involved in sexual affairs. They acknowledged that Christ is God's Son, that we were all God's sons, and that we could all be elevated to the level of pure consciousness of God. I think my parents were relieved that I would be living a clean life.

After two years in the movement, I married and we had a child, pleasing my parents. I wasn't forced out onto the street for 10 or 12 hours to collect money all day long, like a lot of Krishna people. I was in charge of the organization's printing and publishing. My parents thought, "Well, he is involved in the field he went to school for."

I asked my folks, "Why is it that you want to fill the world with more violence by condoning the slaughter of animals?" I convinced them to become vegetarians. They could see my dedication and weren't aware of any hypocrisy because we were getting up at 4 A.M. and maintaining an austere life of commitment to God. They had to respect that.

Everyone rose early. The first service was at 4:30 A.M. and lasted half an hour. Then there were two hours of meditation, chanting on the beads. After that there was a class on the Vedic scriptures from India, and finally breakfast. From there, people went to work, collecting money, working in a candle-making factory, or whatever they did. They came back in the evening for an evening service. Then they went to another class, and finally home.

In the worship service they chanted on beads and worshiped statues. They had food which, by the act of offering, became the body of the deity. There were incantations in a foreign tongue, and a lot of rituals, incense, and songs. I thought this might be the Eastern version of Catholicism, except that we had better answers because we had reincarnation and karma to explain things philosophically. We thought we were far superior.

The philosophy calls for trying to minimize eating and sleeping. The less you eat, the less you sleep, the less you have sex, the more you can purely dedicate yourself to God.

I remember thinking that maybe I could sleep only four hours a night, and tried that for a while, but ultimately my sleep averaged six hours. Then I had to feel guilty! Here I was in a state they call "nescience" (darkness, the opposite of knowledge), lying on the floor for six hours—a complete waste of time when I could have been serving God.

Nonetheless, the regimen gave us a certain amount of contempt toward Christians who tried to talk to us. We didn't accept them even though we professed that we accepted everyone, because we believed ultimately everyone was on the path back to God. Christians were meat eaters, and we figured that vegetarianism was "Point A" of spiritual life. People who couldn't even get on *that* level were hardly human beings not to mention spiritual persons. We noted that even their own commandments say, "Thou shalt not kill," and here they were killing animals. What kind of hypocrisy was this? They were using other forms of life to indulge in sensual pleasures, whereas the human life is meant for spiritual dedication to God.

ISKCON teaches that if you become a vegetarian you'll have fewer violent vibrations since you're not eating violently slaughtered animal flesh. But I saw people in the movement who often got angry and aggressive. On the other hand, I've found people who eat meat who are very dedicated to God, peaceful, and loving.

One thing that the Krishnas could never explain was Christ eating flesh. It is really interesting that they could never write off Christ. They could never say, "Well, He doesn't matter because He's not important." They *know* He is a very important spiritual figure. Most of the time they would say, "Well, it wasn't really fish He was eating; it's just an interpretation of the Greek. It was a fishbread plant," or something like that. The guru (Bhaktivedanta Swami Prabhupada, ISKCON founder) would say, "Well Christ is so high spiritually, He's so perfect, He could eat the whole world." I never knew what that meant. The guru said, "Don't think that you're on the same level as Jesus Christ. He was preaching according to time and circumstance. He was in an area where there were no vegetables."

When I went to Israel, I found that the area where Christ preached around the Sea of Galilee, in Capernaum, was rich in vegetables. So those arguments don't hold at all.

The Krishnas chant over and over again and experience a certain euphoria, a bliss or joy, a high; but I came to realize that this was not necessarily of God. After I became a Christian, I realized that it was definitely *not* of God because the chanting opens a person to control by the organization. It molds your thinking in such a way that you begin to view the world in terms of "us versus them." It's an elitist mentality. "We are chanting Hare Krishna; we are vegetarians; we are the ones who are celibate; we are the only spiritual people on the face of the earth; we are the only enlightened ones; we must bring people to this enlightened stage."

After four and a half years in ISKCON, one thing that made me question it was the way I related to my parents. At one point, after my first child was born, I didn't even want them touching the child because of their karmic vibrations. I was treating them harshly, yet taking money whenever they offered it.

Another incident that started turning me away occurred about the same time—1975 or 1976. The strategy of the movement had changed since I joined. Back in 1971 the idea was to go out and sing on the streets, to chant God's name, and the world would come to understand that we were all brothers under one God. There would be one-world unity that we could usher in by inundating the planet with spiritual vibrations. We really had quite a missionary sense about it.

Then things started changing. The guru said, "OK, this chanting in the streets is still important, but the most important thing is that people are suffering because they are ignorant of God's law. They are committing sin. Because of that sin they are suffering karmic reaction. The way to relieve the suffering is to stop the sinning.

The way to stop the sinning is to give the people knowledge of God and His laws. The knowledge of God and His laws is in my books. So the way to stop the suffering in the world is to distribute these books—to edify the world and help them to be elevated spiritually. To alleviate the suffering in the world, you have to get this knowledge out."

The only problem was that no one wanted to read about a Krishna from India who played with cows and had girlfriends. So we had to disguise what we were passing out. We wouldn't say anything about Krishna. We'd say, "You've heard about meditation and yoga; well, this is about meditation and yoga." And people were still reluctant to part with $5 of their money.

We started to develop more deceptive tactics. We'd say, "We're student teachers and we're working with children. Could you give a donation? Oh, by the way, here's a book." Or, we'd give a person a book and say, "Yeah, we're working all over the world. We're working with kids and helping people. Why don't you give us a donation and keep the book?"

The Krishnas used the short-change technique, which was very popular at O'Hare Airport in Chicago. In fact, it was developed there and in Los Angeles where they would say to someone, "Listen, I've got 20 one-dollar bills and I'm trying to get rid of all these bills. I'm working with children and we have a very good program in getting people involved; we're soliciting people's support to help with these programs for children. Do you have a 20-dollar bill that you could give me for these singles?" The person would hand over a 20-dollar bill and the ISKCON member would peel off 2 one-dollar bills and say, "Well, why don't you let us keep the rest, because we're working with kids, and this is a really good thing we're doing."

Here is a person stopped in the middle of a busy thoroughfare, maybe trying to catch a plane, and usually embarrassed to decline helping children. He may feel like walking away from it, which is what most do.

I've seen Kirshnas tell a serviceman they would change a $50 bill for him and bring back $40 if he was willing to make a $10 donation, and then they would disappear into the washroom for a half hour. We reported this to the guru in India. I thought, "When he hears what's going on, he'll put an end to it." But when the letter came back, the guru said, "Well, the person who reported these activities in the newspaper has used the name *Krishna* many times. This is very good because by reading the name *Krishna*, people will be purified; they will be benefited by hearing the holy name." And then he used the phrase, "By hook or by crook, get them to take the book," and added, "the end justifies the means."

I saw the same kind of philosophy applied in marriages and even in my own marriage. I was taught not to have any kind of sexual contact with my wife except when we wanted to conceive a child, and even then only once a month, and after chanting for eight hours to purify the act. I sometimes resolved this by turning my wife into an object of contempt in order not to have physical feelings for her.

I saw many marriages broken. Of course, the Krishnas would say, "Look how many divorces there are in unspiritual American society." In ISKCON about 75 percent or more of the marriages end in divorce. The children are orphaned, the husband leaves, the wife leaves. Krishna leaders would say, "It's your *own* fault; it's because you're so weak, that you can't be nice to your spouse and at the same time remain celibate."

Then I started questioning. I said, "Is it really my fault, or is there something wrong with the philosophy that creates deceptive soliciting techniques and destroys marriages and home life?"

What capped it off was when I heard about a friend who was about the same age as myself, also a college graduate, an honor graduate from Cornell University. He was intelligent and personable, the head of the New York Krishna temple for many years. I knew him well, and I had heard that he took the order of Sannyasa, considered a high state of achievement in ISKCON. He had reached this advanced state of spirituality by renouncing things of the world: he had never married, and had no home.

One day I was talking with the leader of the Los Angeles temple. He said, "Did you hear what happened to John? He must have been despondent about not meeting his book distribution and collection quotas. He walked into a lake in St. Louis in the middle of January with a pistol in one hand and his chanting beads in the other, and blew his brains out." And I thought, "I don't know what's going on in this movement, but it certainly is very sick."

I told my wife about it and she was marginally sympathetic. I said, "I'm not going to the temple anymore in the morning. I'm going to continue getting up at 4:30, but I'm going to read the

Bible instead." She said, "Well, that's spiritual too."

Anyway, I started to doubt that one could, by austerity, raise himself by his bootstraps to reach a level in which he was free from all material desires. I certainly hadn't seen that in myself, having practiced these principles for nine years. I hadn't seen myself delivered from selfishness, insensitivity, harshness, lust. I looked around in the movement at my brothers and sisters, and they were still affected by these things.

The guru was saying and doing things ostensibly for Krishna, but I saw much of it was for his own glory. I felt I'd been cheated and I wanted a real spiritual teacher. I started to look toward Jesus.

When Swami Prabhupada died, he left 11 of his closest disciples in charge. I thought, "Wait a minute; these guys are supposed to be pure, fully liberated from all material desires, otherwise they can't be gurus. We must have a living guru to liberate us from the material world."

I started saying to myself, "Even after many reincarnations, how many people are really purified and free from material desires?" I would say to people who were in ISKCON, or who were involved in Eastern philosophy, "Even if there were a few who had reached this perfect state, does that seem like an equitable plan of salvation, that out of the billions and billions of people who have walked the face of the earth only a handful would be liberated?"

Basically, we were taught in ISKCON that in reincarnation you have many chances, many lifetimes to come back and reform, to get better and better, evolving to a higher level. But I've never seen *anybody* come to that point. "So does this mean that I'm condemned because I'm not able to live up to God's standard of perfection?" I asked myself. And I started praying.

I had been reading the Bible for a couple of weeks, and one day as I was driving my car, I just started praying. "God, I don't know who You are, but I *know* You are, and I know that I've failed You. I know I'm not perfect, and I'm sorry. I don't want to be condemned. I want Your forgiveness, Your salvation. Please come into my life and make me what I couldn't become on my own."

It was at that point that I felt the presence of Jesus—His love, His acceptance, His mercy, His warmth. I felt forgiven. I had a new lease on life. It was like the first day of my life—a moving experience.

In ISKCON, the more I chanted, the more I was acceptable to God, and one day I would attain salvation and go to the spiritual sky. But Christianity was quite the opposite: I came with an open heart, standing before God in total honesty and saying, "I can't do it on my own. I'm a sinner and I need Christ's help."

As far as reaching people in ISKCON, it's a question of their hearts being ready. I think the battle takes place in the prayer realm. The best thing is to try and get them to think about what they believe and what they lack without Jesus Christ.

Darkness vs. Light

Hare Krishna Says:

"Hare Krishna, Hare Krishna, Krishna, Krishna, Hare, Hare, Hare Rama, Hare Rama, Rama, Rama, Hare, Hare." (great mantra of Hare Krishna)

"Philanthropists who build educational institutions, hospitals, and churches are wasting their time when they could be building Krishna temples instead." (A.C. Bhaktivedanta Prabhupada, *Krishna, Volume 3*)

"Take it from me that a person who considers his family and relatives as his own is an ass." (A.C. Bhaktivedanta Prabhupada, *Krishna, Volume 3*)

"Abandon all varieties of religion and just surrender to me." (Krishna, *Bhagavad-Gita* 18:66)

"They also who worship other gods and make offering with faith ... do verily make offering to me." (Krishna, *Bhagavad-Gita* 9:23)

"To the born, sure is death; to the dead, sure is birth; so for an issue that may not be escaped thou dost not well to sorrow." (Krishna, *Bhagavad-Gita* 2:27)

The Bible Says:

"When you pray, go into your inner room, and when you have shut your door, pray to your Father who is in secret." (Jesus, *Matthew* 6:6)

"While we have opportunity, let us do good to all men, especially to those who are of the household of the faith." (Apostle Paul, *Galatians* 6:10)

"If any one does not provide for his own, and especially for those of his household, he has denied the faith." (Apostle Paul, *1 Timothy* 5:8)

"Be gone, Satan! For it is written, 'You shall worship the Lord your God and serve Him only.'" (Jesus, *Matthew* 4:10)

"You shall not follow other gods, any of the gods of the peoples who surround you ... otherwise the anger of the Lord your God will be kindled against you." (Prophet Moses, *Deuteronomy* 6:14-15)

"Now the end is upon you, and I shall send My anger against you; I shall judge you according to your ways ... then you will know that I am the Lord!" (Jehovah, *Ezekiel* 7:3-4)

SECTION 2
The Religion Trip

13
Allah Failed to Answer Me

*Anonymous
as told to Mark Hannah*

During the sacred month of Ramadan, I felt that I was the holiest man in the world. I wore the Muslim garb and spent hour after hour praising Allah. I tried to do everything that was expected of a devout Muslim. Fasting, praying, almsgiving, repeating the kalima, and hoping to make a pilgrimage to Mecca—these were the central concerns of my life. The mosque was like my second home, so often was I within its precincts and in its minarets.

In the Koran, Allah is depicted as the Creator who is not only far above the world he has made, but is also far from every human

---

Dr. Mark Hannah is associate professor of philosophy of religion and department chairman at Talbot Theological Seminary, La Mirada, California. He also is on the teaching staff of International Students, Inc., an evangelistic ministry to foreign students in the U.S.

being. He keeps an accurate record of our deeds so he can recompense us with final rewards or ultimate punishment on the last day. This knowledge filled my heart with dread, for I knew I had often fallen short of the requirements of true virtue.

According to the belief of many Muslims, when we die, an angel stands ready to assist us. But each one of us has to face judgment alone, on the basis of achievements and failures. At the judgment there is a bridge over which everyone must walk. It is only one-seventh the thickness of a hair. If one's good deeds are greater than his evil deeds, the bridge widens to enable him to go across to heaven. Otherwise, he falls into hell below.

Islam has many adherents in Java, where I have lived all my life. At the age of 12, I resolved to follow Islam with wholehearted determination. I went to the mosque almost every day, and I received instruction in Islam with great eagerness. Of course, I memorized long passages from the Koran, and I learned all of the prescribed ritual prayers. I tried to obey Allah as faithfully as Muhammad did. Nothing was more important to me than preparing for the final judgment. I was constantly preoccupied with fulfilling the will of Allah in my daily affairs.

At the age of 16 I had such a strong desire to become a teacher that I decided to leave home. I was even willing to attend a Christian teachers college in Jakarta. There was an opening for me there—and besides, I was so well established in my Islamic convictions that I had no fear that anything could deflect me from them.

When I arrived at the college and was assigned a room in one of the dormitories, I continued to pray five times a day. This annoyed the other students, especially since I was the only one who did it. Even so, I knew something was missing at the root of my being.

One evening a man came to the dormitory to talk to all the students about Christ. He had a warm smile that radiated an undeniable inner joy. I hated Christians, and so I concealed my feelings of envy at their peace and happiness. Instead of listening with respect, I mocked him. He was a fellow Indonesian, but to me he was an unclean heathen. I intensely resisted his ideas and designed my questions to anger him. But he never lost his composure. He continued to patiently answer my questions. Eventually he left with obvious regret over my belligerence.

After that encounter, I had mixed feelings. I could not shake the image of his kind face from my mind; I knew that he had something in his life that I didn't have. And yet, I was confident he was a purveyor of error and an enemy of God. I was especially disturbed by his quotation from the Bible: "Jesus said to him, 'I am the way, and the truth, and the life; no one comes to the Father, but through Me'" (John 14:6). The claim that Christ is the only way angered me more than anything. But it also made me uncertain about my own beliefs. The fact that the students who were sincere Christians lived good lives increased my confusion. One person in the dormitory greatly attracted me to Christianity. He kept the Christian faith before me not only in words, but in his character and actions.

I was religious but not happy, even when I did what was expected of me by Islam. I couldn't forget what I had heard that evening: the Bible teaches that all of us are sinners, and yet God loves us, and through Christ He can forgive and save us.

There was so much I didn't understand about Jesus. I had heard that "the wages of sin is death, but the free gift of God is eternal life in Christ Jesus our Lord" (Romans 6:23), but I did not know what it meant. My Christian classmate told me that his joy came from trusting in Jesus as his Saviour and Lord. When he told me that God demonstrated His love by coming in the person of Christ to give His life on the cross for our sins, I was amazed. I had never heard anything like that.

I wondered if all of this could be true. I thought about it very much—in fact, I thought about it for three months. I then decided to go to church with my classmate. At that meeting I was more impressed by the attitude of the Christians. They astonished me with their kindness.

I continued to go to church because of the sincerity I saw in the people there. One day my friend could not go with me, so he told me to take from his wallet whatever money I needed for transportation. My friend was a *true friend* and the first to demonstrate God's love toward me. After several months of turmoil over the question of the truth of the Christian faith, I finally concluded that I must put my entire trust in Christ as my Saviour and Lord.

It is impossible to describe the change that Christ brought in my life. I felt that a great burden had been removed from my heart. I experienced the same joy that other Christians had. Jesus said that

He came that we might have life and have it in fullness (see John 10:10). Now I discovered what He meant.

I discovered that I was no longer afraid to die and meet God. When I had been a faithful Muslim, I never lost my fear of death. But when I believed that Christ conquered death by His resurrection, the fear of death disappeared. Now I know that "to live is Christ, and to die is gain" (Philippians 1:21), for to depart from this life is to be with Christ which is far better. I also learned that I am in this world because God has something special for me to do. His purpose for my life has become my main motivation and goal.

My heart had previously been dominated by fear and hate, but Christ cleansed me of my corrupt attitudes and replaced them with assurance and love. I had a great desire to tell my people about the wonderful Saviour I had met. I went home and told my adoptive parents about my faith in Christ. My natural father had died when I was only four, and while I was still young I had been adopted. When my new parents learned that I was sincere about my commitment to Christ, they used a variety of pressures to reclaim me for Islam. They were fearful that I would influence the rest of the children in the family. They denounced the Christian faith as evil and foolish.

Every Sunday my mother tried to keep me from going to church by asking me to do something for her at home. So Saturday night I would ask her what she wanted me to do the following day. And when she would tell me what task I was to perform on Sunday, I would arise early in the morning and finish it in time to go to church. My mother became very angry one day and said, "Son, you have to choose between me and Jesus Christ."

I replied, "I am sorry, Mother, I have to follow Christ. It does not mean that I hate you; I love you, but I must put Christ first in my life."

She kept silent. Then I told her that I was going to become a Christian preacher. My father and mother both stood against my decision. He was the ambassador to a European country, and he could give me many advantages. The choice before me was clear. They said that I must choose them or Christ. They warned me that I would lose all the privileges and opportunities that they could give me: a European education, a car, travel in the West.

Conflict raged in my mind. I wondered what would happen to me if they disowned me. Where would I get the money I needed for my education? Was I being a fool to give up all the advantages I knew were in the palm of my hand? I was still young and dependent on my parents' support. And I did not want to hurt them, for they had been kind to me and I loved them very much. I had to determine whether or not Christ was worth the renunciation of all things. After careful consideration and agonizing reflection, I decided to let nothing be more important to me than Christ. There was no alternative, for He gave all for me—He died for me and He is coming again for me. I knew I must put Him above everyone. By the grace of God, I made my decision.

I finished my studies at the teachers college and then taught for three years. After that I went to study in a theological school so I could prepare to preach the Gospel of Christ.

Some of my Muslim friends ridiculed me for becoming a believer in Christ. One who said I was insane agreed later to go to church with me. He wanted to find out what it was that attracted me. He too was overwhelmed by the love of Christ and put his trust in Him. To this day he is serving Christ.

I went to various parts of Java to preach about Jesus Christ, and I was amazed as I witnessed hundreds of people turning to Him. Most of them had never heard the wonderful truth that God loves them and forgives every sin through Christ.

A number have had deep transformations in their lives from believing in Christ. Before they came to know Christ, some were leaders in Muslim communities and knew Islamic literature and practices. They had seen Islam's most sacred city when they made their pilgrimage to Mecca. Yet they found something in Christ that Islam could not give them. Only genuine Christians know the peace and joy that comes from fellowship with God and with other believers in Christ.

Before, I was always in a state of anxiety and frustration. But in Christ I have assurance and rest. The most important thing to me is the love of Christ and the love He puts in the hearts of those who sincerely believe in Him. True Christians love Muslims. If anyone calls himself a Christian and hates anyone else, he is self-deceived, for he does not truly know Christ.

When I became a believer in Christ, I lost my family and relatives. But Christ has taken care of me, and I have found that I have hundreds of brothers and sisters all around me—and many more all over the world.

Some time after I became a believer, I went to see a former Christian teacher. I had given him much trouble, for I was a proud, argumentative student. As soon as he saw me, he came and embraced me. He had nothing but love and forgiveness in his heart. "You were my foe, but now you are my friend," he said.

I have thought again and again about that statement—"my foe, but now my friend." My classmate had been a faithful friend and now my former teacher had become a wonderful friend. I realized that the sincerity of their friendship was a reality because of the ultimate friend whom they knew and loved—the Lord Jesus Christ.

The words of Jesus tell us that those who love Him are not merely His servants but are His friends (see John 15:15). And now I belonged to Him—mind, body, and soul—because in Him I had discovered the one true friend who would never leave me or forsake me (see Hebrews 13:5).

Darkness vs. Light

Islam Says:

"They are unbelievers who say, 'God is the Messiah, Mary's son.'" (Mohammed, *Koran*, Sura 5:19)

"We believe in God, and the revelation given to us and to Abraham Isma'il, Isaac, Jacob, and the tribes, and that given to Moses and Jesus . . . we make no distinction between one and another of them." (Mohammed, *Koran*, Sura 2:136)

"When the angels said, 'Mary, God gives thee good tidings of a Word from Him whose name is Messiah, Jesus, son of Mary; high honored shall he be in this world and the next, near stationed to God." (Mohammed, *Koran*, Sura 3:40)

"They did not slay him, neither crucified him; only a likeness of that was shown to them." (Mohammed, *Koran*, Sura 4:156)

"Whoever goeth right, it is only for his own soul that he goeth right; and whoever errs, errs only to his hurt. No laden soul can bear another's load." (Mohammed, *Koran*, Sura 17:15)

The Bible Says:

"Behold, the virgin shall be with child, and shall bear a son, and they shall call His name Immanuel, which translated means 'God with us.'" (Apostle Matthew, *Matthew* 1:23)

"It is not Moses who has given you the bread out of heaven, but it is My Father who gives you the true bread." / "I am the bread of life; he who comes to Me shall not hunger, and he who believes in Me shall never thirst." (Jesus, *John* 6:32, 35)

"God, after He spoke long ago to the fathers in the prophets in many portions and in many ways, in these last days has spoken to us by His Son, whom He appointed heir of all things, through whom also He made the world." (*Hebrews* 1:1-2)

"Greater love has no one than this, that one lay down his life for his friends." / "I was dead, and behold, I am alive forevermore, and I have the keys of death and of Hades." (Jesus, *John* 15:13; *Revelation* 1:18)

"All of us like sheep have gone astray. Each of us has turned to his own way; but the Lord has caused the iniquity of us all to fall on Him." (Prophet Isaiah, *Isaiah* 53:6)

"I am only a mortal the like of you; it is revealed to me that your God is one God." (Mohammed, *Koran,* Sura 18:110)

"So believe in God and His Messengers, and say not, 'Three.' Refrain; better is it for you. God is only one God." (Mohammed, *Koran,* Sura 4:169)

"Glorify Thou Me together with Thyself, Father, with the glory which I had with Thee before the world was." (Jesus, *John* 17:5)

"When the kindness of God our Saviour and His love for mankind appeared, He saved us, not on the basis of deeds which we have done in righteousness, but according to His mercy, by the washing of regeneration and renewing of the Holy Spirit, whom He poured out upon us richly through Jesus Christ our Saviour." (Apostle Paul, *Titus* 3:4-6)

14
I Worshiped a Million Gods
by Rita Sairsingh

For most of my life I was a devout Hindu, worshiping Rama, Krishna, Siva, and others of the thousands of gods transplanted by my ancestors from India to the island nation of Trinidad. But there never were enough of them to help me!

In my childhood I was never close to my parents. I remember Mother getting sick when I was very young. She became an invalid, bedridden and unable to move. My father simply brought home another mom to look after all of us kids.

I enjoyed needlework—any kind of sewing—very much, and I especially liked going to school. Sometimes during those early years, in order to get away from my stepmother, I would slip off to sit under the trees and listen to the birds, dreaming how life would one day be for me.

On my twelfth birthday, my father announced that he could no longer afford to send me to school. I would have to stay home and help with the household chores. I cried and begged my friends to talk with my father, but it was no use. Even my sewing lessons were cancelled.

I was married at age 15, under less than romantic circumstances.

Rita Sairsingh was a homemaker in Trinidad when she told her story.

My father announced he had found the man, and all arrangements had been made.

A week after the wedding I discovered my husband was a chronic alcoholic. He was also a heavy smoker, and in lots of ways a rather unbearable man; but I submitted myself to what seemed my inevitable lot in life and tried hard to build a home.

Perhaps, under the circumstances, the marriage never had a chance. We separated many times; and in 1953, with five children to support, I left my husband for good and plunged deeply into the mysteries of the Hindu religion. I thought surely one of the more than 35 million Hindu gods would be able to give me peace of mind.

I became obsessed with the idea of attaining samadhi, the superconscious state. I corresponded with priests in India, wrote articles, and followed their instructions to the letter. Some of my poems were published in their monthly magazine.

Knowing the Hindu language, I sang for the villagers on special occasions. I taught the children in various homes, and I held services from house to house. Eventually I became known as something of a Hindu priestess among the people of my village.

My treasure was the Gita, a Hindu religious book which I kept on an altar in a special room of my house. Never would I go into that room—or permit another to go there—with shoes on.

The Hindu holy men had told me that if I chanted a special prayer 50 million times, I would find salvation. Day after day I went into my prayer room, and sometimes way into the night I chanted my prayer over and over, counting beads in order to keep a record.

Years passed. One day, suddenly, I had an attack of facial paralysis and was rushed to the hospital in great pain. Taking my treasured god Krishna with me, I put him on a shelf near the head of my bed and prayed most of the time, but I continued to suffer. Strange noises pounded in my head, and I became deaf in my left ear. I also developed a speech defect.

Finally discharged from the hospital, but still with the ear and speech defects and with the understanding that I would return to the hospital periodically for injections, I called a special fast and wrote urgent letters to the priests in India. But everything seemed to get worse, and I began to worry about dying and what would happen to my children.

One day in 1962 my teenage son came home bubbling with joy and saying he had wonderful news. A boy at school had told him Jesus could heal me and give me peace of mind. I was not pleased at his mentioning the name of Jesus, and I warned him to stay away from Christians.

But the next day he came home even more excited and said, "I don't care what you say, Mom, I've given myself to Jesus. He's my Saviour. He's washed away my sins, and everything in the whole world has changed. I love Jesus, Mom. I'm now a Christian, and the other Christians say you're wasting your time with all those dead gods."

"Son, how can you say such things?" I was horrified! My very own son! "You've got to stop this. What will people say?"

I pretended to pay no further attention; I would not talk to him about it. But his enthusiasm, joy, and obvious transformation made me think. It all seemed very odd. After many years of religious searching, I had found nothing; but my son, in a matter of hours, had given every indication of having found the peace and happiness I had been dreaming about for a lifetime.

I became restless, especially at night; and I often thought about my son's Jesus, though I really knew nothing about Him.

One morning I sat down before my altar to meditate. Trying to light the incense, I felt a strange yearning in my heart, and my lips were sealed so that I couldn't speak. I could only weep. For a long time I cried for the ache in my heart and for the gods that I could no longer worship.

Getting to my feet, I went over to another corner of my room. "O God," I said aloud, "where are You, God? I'm so confused. Please help me, Lord. Please."

After a time I felt better. I wiped my tears, and for the first time in years I went through the day without worshiping my gods.

Arising early the next morning, I felt an unseen presence in my room. I looked behind me. No one was there. But I heard a voice saying, "I am the way, the truth, and the life" (John 14:6). Over and over I heard that voice. When my son woke up, I told him what I had heard. "Don't worry, Mom, that's just Jesus talking to you," he assured me.

I didn't say much, but inside I discovered a growing excitement. There wasn't fear; rather, I felt as if I were on the brink of a great discovery.

"Mom, you've got to quit reading the Gita," my son said. "Read the Bible. Here, you can read mine."

One verse in the Bible caught my attention: "It is appointed for men to die once, but after this comes judgment" (Hebrews 9:27). To a Hindu, who had constantly been taught that life is one continuing, reincarnating cycle, that statement was startling. I had always thought my troubles were caused by some mistake of a former life, and I had prayed for years that things would be better in my next life.

That evening I talked with my son about the strange Scripture, and he explained about the Creation, man's first sin, God's love, and the sending of Jesus Christ into the world as the Saviour.

Day after day I continued to read the Bible. One evening my son invited me to go with him to a Christian service.

"Oh, no, Son. I can't do that."

"Sure you can, Mom. Please."

I finally agreed to go for one visit. I was nervous, wondering who was watching and asking myself what my Hindu friends would say.

The church songs were beautiful, and the minister preached about Jesus and God's love. All during the service I felt as though someone were whispering in my ear, "This is your night—your moment. You *must* go down and pray."

The preacher finally gave the invitation, and I walked forward and knelt. A young girl explained to me more fully what it meant to be saved and to serve the Lord Jesus. I poured out my soul to God, and I asked Him to have mercy on me, a sinner. Joy poured into my heart, and the presence of Christ became so real that I felt as if I could reach out and touch Him.

News of my conversion spread like wind through the village. Priests, relatives, friends—even Muslims—became alarmed. They called me a fool. One Hindu priest came to the house and said that Christ and all Christians were dogs. But the Lord gave me strength, and I prayed for that priest.

Since my conversion, my mother and all of my children have been saved. I work for the Lord much of the time. And now my son is a minister of the Gospel.

I thank God for having called me out of darkness into the light of His marvelous love. I know there is no greater miracle in the world than being redeemed by Jesus for eternity.

Darkness vs. Light

Hinduism Says:

"In whatever way men approach me, even so do I receive them, for even the paths men take from every side are mine." (Lord Krishna, *Bhagavad-Gita* IV, 11)

"When all desires which once entered his heart are undone, then does the mortal become immortal, then he obtains Brahman." (*Upanishads, Brihad-Aranyaka, Fourth Adhyaya, Fourth Brahmaba*, 6)

"To the Hindu philosophers, nothing is more irreligious than a holier-than-thou attitude—an attitude which of necessity provides the driving force of evangelism." (Krishnalal Shridharani, *My India, My America*)

"The theist and the atheist, the skeptic and the agnostic may all be Hindus if they accept the Hindu system of culture and life." (Radhakrishnan, *The Hindu View of Life*)

"It was more than I could believe that Jesus was the only incarnate son of God. If Jesus was like God . . . then all men were like God and could be God himself!" (Mahatma Gandhi, *Autobiography*)

The Bible Says:

"Enter by the narrow gate; for the gate is wide, and the way is broad that leads to destruction, and many are those who enter by it. For the gate is small, and the way is narrow that leads to life, and few are those who find it." (Jesus, *Matthew* 7:13-14)

"The wages of sin is death, but the free gift of God is eternal life in Christ Jesus our Lord." (Apostle Paul, *Romans* 6:23)

"Knowing the fear of the Lord, we persuade men." / "We are ambassadors for Christ, as though God were entreating through us; we beg you on behalf of Christ, be reconciled to God." (Apostle Paul, *2 Corinthians* 5:11, 20)

"Woe to those who call evil good, and good evil; who substitute darkness for light, and light for darkness." / "They have rejected the Law of the Lord of hosts." (Prophet Isaiah, *Isaiah* 5:20, 24)

"There is but one God, the Father, from whom are all things, and we exist for Him; and one Lord, Jesus Christ, by whom are all things, and we exist through Him." (Apostle Paul, *1 Corinthians* 8:6)

15
Zen Buddhism Blinded Me

by Lit-sen Chang

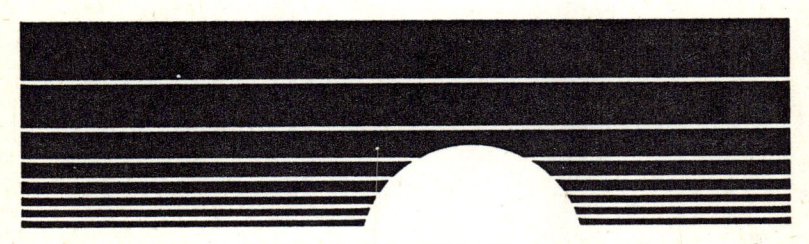

During my boyhood, I studied Buddhist literature with my mother in China and was much inspired by her wonderful stories about her vision of Buddha. While my mother was a believer of the Pure Land sect, my father practiced Zen. His raptures in the experience of *satori* ("enlightenment") and his daily "beatific vision" over death and life quite convinced me.

Later I was proud of my own experiences of *satori:* I had a strong sense of airiness, of increasing serenity, of "returning home," a conviction of rightness in all actions, a feeling of exaltation, and a joy as if over death and life.

When our war capital Chungking was on the verge of ruin from endless bombing by the Japanese, one of my colleagues asked me with surprise, "Why are you still serene, as if nothing disturbed you?"

"Zen!" I replied with a proud smile.

When news of my mother's death reached me in Chungking, I

Dr. Lit-sen Chang has for many years lectured on missions at colleges around the USA. From 1956 to 1980 he lectured frequently at Gordon Divinity School and Gordon-Conwell Theological Seminary, South Hamilton, Massachusetts and in 1980 was cited as "Distinguished Lecturer in Missions, Emeritus." He lives in Lexington, Massachusetts.

Zen Buddhism Blinded Me / 115

did not shed a tear. For in Zen, Buddha nature, or the true-self, transcends all duality and is therefore above birth and death. As a result, Zen became even more fascinating to me.

After World War II, in view of the great devastation and upheaval of my nation and of the world, I had a great concern about mankind's future. I believed the hope of mankind and peace on earth were to be found in the East rather than in the West, so I claimed the universal relevance of our religion. For this purpose, I resigned from political activities and founded a university as an initial step.

When I was elected the first president of King-nan University, a group of prominent scholars in Chinese culture and philosophy cooperated with me to promote a revival of Oriental religions and civilizations. In 1949, a famous university in India invited me to give a series of lectures on the general theme "The Destiny of Asia." I accepted, intending to realize my ambition. But in a mysterious way a diversion to Java changed the whole course of my life.

My family and I left Hong Kong in 1949 after Christmas and arrived in Djakarta in January 1950. We found a house in Semarang next to a church which was under construction. Later I was invited to attend its dedication service. I went with a sense of pride at being invited to sit among social dignitaries and government representatives.

During the dedication service the words of the preacher failed to impress me, but the power of the Holy Spirit in the prayertime deeply touched me. This was the turning point of my life, for since that occasion, my attitude toward Jesus and His church has miraculously changed.

His Spirit began to work mysteriously in my life; I could not stop going to church. In fact, I was so thirsty day and night for Jesus, the Living Water of Life, I would go several hundred miles to attend an evangelistic meeting.

From 1951, I began to read the Bible regularly. As God called me out of darkness into His marvelous light, He removed the veil which was over my heart. Amazingly, I cried when I read the Bible or even a simple Gospel leaflet.

The Bible was not new to me. I had read it the first time at Shanghai Baptist University, but it had been with repulsion and hatred; and as a result, I deserted the school and later supported

116 / Escape from Darkness

the anti-Christian movement by contributing articles to newspapers. When I was co-founder of an Association of Comparative Religions, I read the Bible again in order to show my impartiality to all religions. I read it in ignorance, because it was a closed book to my arrogant mind. The third time, after my conversion, I read the Bible tearfully, as a prodigal son coming home to meet his loving father. This was not a short-lived emotion. It lasted for many months, and continues to recur.

This is a strong evidence of the Bible truth that "the Word of the Cross is to those who are perishing foolishness, but to us who are being saved it is the power of God" (1 Corinthians 1:18). It further proves that until "the blood of Jesus His Son cleanses us from all sin" (1 John 1:7) and until "the God of our Lord Jesus Christ, the Father of glory, may give to you a spirit of wisdom and of revelation in the knowledge of Him . . . that the eyes of your heart may be enlightened" (Ephesians 1:17-18), we can never have genuine satori or open our "third eye," as Zen teaches.

After World War II, Zen became widely known in Europe and America. Zen found its place in the West as a serious study for three principle groups, as the American Alan Watts observed. In philosophical circles, Zen has special relevance to those who are looking for a step beyond the impotent insights of logical positivism. Among scientists, Zen has special appeal to psychotherapists. In the world of art, Zen has indirectly influenced American architecture and Japanese ceramics. Since Zen is markedly different from other forms of Buddhism, and from other religions as well, it has aroused the curiosity of many who would not ordinarily look to the impractical East for practical wisdom. Once such curiosity is aroused, it is not easy to set it at rest, for minds weary of conventional religion and philosophy are particularly fascinated with Zen.

R.H. Blyth contends: "Zen is the most precious possession of Asia. With its beginning in India, development in China, and practical application in Japan, it is today the strongest power in the world. It is a world-power, for in so far as man lives at all, he lives in Zen. Wherever there is poetical action, a religious aspiration, a heroic thought, a union of the Nature within a man and the nature without, there is Zen" (*Zen in English Literature and Oriental Classics*).

In this troubled world Zen is not without some appealing

features. It opposes rationalism and humanism. According to Zen adherents, "Mere scholasticism or mere sacerdotalism . . . will never create a living faith. The intellect is useful in its place; when it tries to cover the whole field of religion, it dries up the source of life. Zen transcends logic and overrides the tyranny and misrepresentation of ideas" (D.T. Suzuki, *Selected Writings*).

Another observes: "The present time is the age of humanism in which the human being is the scale of all things. The humanism of the enlightenment in the 18th century liberated him from political and economic bondage to the ruling class . . . [but] humanism can't liberate man completely or satisfactorily" (Ogata, *Zen for the West*). In depicting the plight of modern man, Zenists seemingly have some penetrating insights. But since this movement is only a turning inward, it still remains ensnared in the very pit of the humanism it claims to oppose.

It teaches self-denial and "great death." According to its doctrines on wu-chu (nonabiding) and wu-nieng (no thought), "Our individual consciousness, merged into the unconscious, must become like the body of a dead man." / "The unconscious is to let 'Thy will be done' and not to assert my own. All the doings and happenings, including thoughts and feelings, which I have or which come to me, are of the divine will as long as there are on my part no clingings, no hankerings, and my mind is wholly disconnected with things of the past, present and future" (Suzuki, *Selected Writings*).

The teaching of "great death" is to awaken the "inner life of man." Indeed, the characteristic of modern civilization, as the French philosopher Bernanos puts it, is "a universal conspiracy against the inner life of man." This is an existential, dialectical movement through which self-denial is simultanously self-election—choice of one's self as infinite and absolute—and by which, we are told, one attains eternal salvation.

Zen casts some dim light on the way of life. Some Zen scholars quote or employ biblical phrases to illustrate their position or to express their aspiration about the way of life, though they frequently wrest the texts and pervert the truth; e.g., "It is at once the life, the truth and the way." / "The Truth shall make you free." / "He that loseth his life shall find it." / "Take no thought to the morrow." / "Before Abraham was, I am." / "Except a man be born again, he cannot see the Kingdom of God."

Modern Zen writers have deliberately borrowed biblical terminologies to express what they cannot communicate otherwise. This proves that the Christian truths are far more adequate than the messages of Zen, even though Zen so often distorts these truths to meet its own ends. Even though there is some truth in Zen, it is from general revelation which does not convey to man any absolutely reliable knowledge of God, nor acquaint man with the only way of salvation.

So in fact Zen is a peculiar and subtle form of atheism. It denies the infinity and transcendence of a living, personal God by identifying Him with nature. All visible objects thus become feeling modifications of self-existence, unconscious and impersonal essence, which may be called God, Nature, the Absolute, Oneness, Suchness, or Tathata. Zen robs God of His sovereignty by denuding Him of His power of self-determination in relation to the world.

But as it adopts the language of theism and employs Bible verses, Zen may generate a certain mystic piety. Moreover, statements are embellished with the charms of seductive eloquence and become the rival of Christian theism. As Suzuki writes, "The highest thing is to be comprehended or intuited prior to time. It is Godhead who is even before it became God and created the world." / "In the beginning there is 'the Word,' but in the beginningless beginning, there is the Godhead who is nameless and no-word."

What Zen offered me was merely a technique of self-intoxication, or a sense of false security. As the late Dr. Carl G. Jung wrote in a foreword of Dr. Suzuki's *An Introduction to Zen Buddhism,* "I treat satori as a psychological problem .... The imagination itself is a psychic occurrence. The man who has enlightenment or alleges that he has it thinks in any case that he is enlightened ... even if he were to lie." Jung pointed out satori was a result of "many years of the most strenuous devastation of rational understanding."

For many years I thought I was enlightened and boasted of righteousness, but at conversion I found myself confronted by a revelation of God which led me to see His majesty and my own sinful nature. Then I said with Isaiah: "Woe is me! For I am ruined, because I am a man of unclean lips, and I live among a people of unclean lips, for my eyes have seen the King, the Lord of hosts" (6:5). I cried out in repentance with Job: "I have heard of Thee by the hearing of the ear: but now my eye sees Thee. Therefore I retract, and I repent in dust and ashes" (Job 42:5-6).

The tragic mistake I made was that I identified Christianity with Western culture and was ignorant of the fact that Christianity has an Asian origin and is not a religion merely for the West. With this wrong view, I began to regard the world in a distorted way. When I became disillusioned with the West, I thought the way of salvation should be found in the East; but did not realize that "salvation belongs to the Lord" (Psalm 3:8). It comes from heaven, not from West or from East. It comes from above, not from "within" as the Zen teaches. It is of no profit to look within. "I know that nothing good dwells in me" (Romans 7:18). "Unless one is born again, he cannot see the kingdom of God" (John 3:3); nor can he really see his own nature and know his own heart which "is more deceitful than all else and is desperately sick" (Jeremiah 17:9).

The Lord still beckons and stretches His arms to all who seek Him. He still says: "I am the way, and the truth, and the life; no one comes to the Father but through Me" (John 14:6). "Come unto Me, all [Zen-Buddhists, existentialists, death-of-God theologians, beatniks, hippies, LSD addicts] who are weary and are heavy laden, and I will give you rest" (Matthew 11:28). The Cross still stands in the midst of our dilemma as our only hope and glory.

The Gospel of Christ ought to be accepted only because it is the truth, the way, and the life; because it breaks through all human misconceptions and vain imaginations; because it is the only cure for human sins, and the answer to all human problems; and because it confronts mankind with the ultimate reality of God.

The author, called out of pagan darkness into God's marvelous light, presents this witness to readers so they might also come to know the true God, the true Saviour, and true way of liberation.

Darkness vs. Light

Zen Buddhism Says:

"Anything that has the resemblance of an external authority is rejected by Zen. Absolute faith is placed in man's own inner being." (D.T. Suzuki, *Introduction to Zen Buddhism*)

"Zen teaches nothing. Whatever teachings there are in Zen, they come out of one's own mind." (D.T. Suzuki, *Introduction to Zen Buddhism*)

"Zen has no God to worship, no ceremonial rites to observe, no future abode to which the dead are destined." (D.T. Suzuki, *Introduction to Zen Buddhism*)

"[Christian] conversion is held to come to essentially depraved man from an external God, while Satori is the realization of one's own inmost nature." (Alan Watts, *The Way of Liberation in Zen*)

"We can never decide definitely whether a person is really enlightened or whether he merely imagines it; we have no criterion of this." (Carl G. Jung, *Introduction to Zen Buddhism* "Foreword," by D.T. Suzuki)

The Bible Says:

"The world through its wisdom did not know God." / "Your faith should not rest on the wisdom of men, but on the power of God." (Apostle Paul, *1 Corinthians* 1:21; 2:5)

"I know, O Lord, that a man's way is not in himself; nor is it in a man who walks to direct his steps." (Prophet Jeremiah, *Jeremiah* 10:23)

"God is spirit, and those who worship Him must worship in spirit and truth." / "An hour is coming, in which all who are in the tombs shall hear His voice, and shall come forth; those who did the good deeds to a resurrection of life, those who committed the evil deeds to a resurrection of judgment." (Jesus, *John* 4:24; 5:28-29)

"There is none righteous, not even one; there is none who understands, there is none who seeks for God; all have turned aside, together they have become useless." (Apostle Paul, *Romans* 3:10-12)

"These things I have written to you who believe in the name of the Son of God, in order that you may know that you have eternal life." (Apostle John, *1 John* 5:13)

"In the West, 'yes' is 'yes' and 'no' is 'no'; 'yes' can never be 'no' or vice versa. The East makes 'yes' slide over to 'no' and 'no' to 'yes'; there is no hard and fast division between 'yes' and 'no.' It is in the nature of life that it is so. It is only in logic that the division is ineradicable. Logic is human-made to assist in utilitarian activities." (D.T. Suzuki, "Lectures On Zen Buddhism," in *Zen Buddhism and Psychoanalysis*, by Erich Fromm)

"Woe to those . . . who substitute bitter for sweet, and sweet for bitter! Woe to those who are wise in their own eyes." (Prophet Isaiah, *Isaiah* 5:20-21) / "The mature . . . have their senses trained to discern good and evil." (*Hebrews* 5:14)

SECTION 3
The Godless Trip

16
My Life as an Atheist

William J. Murray as told to James R. Adair

It was early October 1960 when my mother, Madalyn Murray (O'Hair), began her campaign deeply involving me to remove prayer and Bible reading from public schools. She had returned from France with my younger half brother Garth, 6, and me, 14, after failing to gain citizenship in the Soviet Union through the Russian embassy in Paris. She despised the United States and its free enterprise system, and the Soviets must have sensed that, with such an attitude, she would do them more good back in the United

---

William J. Murray, a central figure in litigation that resulted in prayer and Bible reading being removed from public schools, lives in Houston, Texas and today is campaigning to have the decision reversed, after having rejected his atheistic beliefs and receiving Christ as his Saviour and Lord.

States. In any event, Nikita Khrushchev or some other high ranking official denied her citizenship, and we returned to Baltimore. A day or so after our arrival, Mother drove me to Woodburn Junior High School to enroll me belatedly for the fall term.

But, understandably, it took a full hour for the counselor to understand why we were actually there. For that early morning as we walked down the hallway, Mother turned red and then purple at seeing some students pledging allegiance to the flag and others praying or reading from the Bible. So upon entering the counselor's office, she began a tirade that embarrassed me as I sat looking at the floor. Finally, the counselor leaned forward and spat out these words:

"Lady, I can't help you. I didn't make the policy; I can't change anything. If you don't like the prayers and Bible reading in classrooms, why don't you just sue!"

He should never have made that suggestion. When we arrived home, Mother was still angry. "We can't have this," she raved. "If they had allowed us to live in the Soviet Union, where we wouldn't have to pray and could practice the politics we like, everything would be fine. We have only one choice: change this country so we don't have to pray and hear the Bible read!"

The first thing she did was write a letter to the president of the school board, demanding that prayer and Bible reading be stopped. Or, she threatened, "I'm going to take my son out of school!" She did take me out of school for about 16 or 17 days, and I'm sure they missed me terribly—the system had only 125,000 students!

Then she fired off a letter to a newspaper, telling of her action. A reporter came out for an interview, resulting in publicity that went from that paper across the country through the various news media. The paper splashed a big picture of me and one of my mother alongside the story; underneath my picture was the word, "Atheist," and beneath my mother's picture, "Atheist's mother." Mother immediately phoned the newspaper—but only to tell them they had misspelled *Madalyn!*

Things really started happening. It seemed as if every dissident in the United States, every God-hater, every hater of democracy, every hater of free enterprise saw that story and loved it! One wealthy Kansas farmer, an atheist and nudist, sent Mother a check

124 / Escape from Darkness

for $5,000 and urged her to keep her cause going. Others wrote letters of encouragement and sent money in many instances.

Mother reveled in it all. "Here I've been involved in so many causes—first, the Socialist Party, then the Socialist Labor Party, the Socialist Worker Party, and the Communist Party, but never was I able to get up to the place where I was Number One," she said in effect. "Now look at this—I have a cause all my own. I am now Number One!"

Soon Mother filed suit in a lower district court to remove prayer and Bible reading from public schools. She contended, on my behalf, that I had been subjected to taunts and physical abuse in school because of my objection to the morning exercises. The Baltimore school board rule, adopted in 1905, provided for "reading, without comment, of a chapter from the Bible, and/or use of the Lord's Prayer." This, Mother's suit argued, was in violation of the First and Fourteenth Amendments relating to "the principle of separation between church and state, and placed in doubt and question our morality, good citizenship, and good faith by placing a premium on belief as against nonbelief in God."

A lot of people laughed at her. "No judge will dare put prayer out of schools. Why, the Bible was one of the original textbooks, and if they didn't want it in public schools they would have said so in the Constitution!" That's how some people felt about it.

But after going from court to court, case No. 119 came before the black-robed men on the Supreme Court, and on June 17, 1963 they looked down from their high benches and rendered an 8-1 decision that made my mother the happiest woman in the land. "We agree with this champion of liberty, this great constitutionalist!" they said in effect. "Bible-reading and prayer recitation in public schools are indeed unconstitutional!"

The Supreme Court decision hit Congressmen like a bombshell. Rep. Alvin O'Konski of Wisconsin said, "If it's illegal in the schools, then it [prayer] must be even more so for the members of Congress. It's too bad too because nine times out of ten, the prayer is the best thing Congress does each day!" Senator Strom Thurmond of South Carolina called the decision "another major triumph for the forces of secularism and atheism."

An atheist like my mother, I certainly wasn't unhappy about the decision. I myself had been caught up in revolutionary and atheistic activities. I was active in the SDS (Students for a

Democratic Society) and knew members of the Weather Underground. Mother and I helped open the first Communist Party bookstore outside of New York—the New Era Bookstore in Baltimore.

It wasn't long after that that our family broke up. I launched out on my own, leaving Mother to her atheistic cause. I worked my way through school, then got involved in aviation. I worked first for Quantas Airways, then for Pan American, American, and finally as an operations manager for Braniff. At 18, I married a Jewish girl but the marriage ended a few years later. I learned that a worker in our society could get a fair shake; I got a number of promotions and pay increases along the way. I had been taught that the American system was all wrong. My mother usually didn't hold a job for more than a few months; she was practicing her atheism, her own goals, and eventually she would be fired. "I was a threat to my supervisor with my superior intelligence," she would say. Since my father had abandoned us when I was quite young, I felt sorry for poor Mom.

But now I was learning that all was not wrong in American business—good workers could get promotions. I also learned that you could go into an election booth and vote for the candidates of your choice for better government; I had not been taught this by my mother, as she herself wrote in her own name!

I finally concluded, as I looked out on the American scene, that there were two groups of nuts: people who believed in God and talked about it, and the group of nuts who didn't believe in God and talked about it. Everybody else just worked for a living and didn't pay any attention one way or the other!

In the years after I left home, I had little contact with my mother. Occasionally she would phone me when she needed something. In 1975 she told me she *needed* me, to help her build up her faltering business. "Your new stepfather in the last five years has taken to drink, and now he has cancer. I can't depend on him anymore," she said. "Bill, I desperately need your help."

I finally decided to go to Austin, Texas and take over her ailing business of promoting atheism. Over a period of about 18 months we went from a gross income of about $2,000 a month to almost $30,000. We moved from three rooms in a frame house to a modern office complex, with a computer and about 20 employees.

But I began to realize that my mother's leftist, atheistic

movement was not for me. In my 13 years away from her influence, I had come to love the United States and the freedom we have as a people. I finally decided I wanted nothing more to do with trying to destroy what I had come to appreciate. It wasn't an easy decision. To help my nation, I had to hurt my family. I began to feel torn apart, and turned to excessive drinking. I couldn't stand being the son of the most hated woman in the land, the woman who was campaigning to get the chaplain out of the U.S. Senate, to bar ministers and rabbis from counseling in hospitals, to remove "In God We Trust" from coins.

I spent some time pretty much off the beaten path, running a bookstore that seldom had a customer. By this time I knew that humanism and atheism and Communism didn't work; all these movements did was to destroy families and nations. But what did work? There in my bookstore I searched, reading about Mohammed, Buddha, Confucius, and Jesus. One book that fascinated me was Taylor Caldwell's *Dear and Glorious Physician* (Doubleday, 1959), a novel about Lucanus (Luke), a young Greek physician who hated God but finally came to know the Lord. This made a lasting impression on me.

In 1978, while in Hawaii working on a magazine, I met my wife, Valerie, a Christian. You'd have to ask her why she married me. I wasn't a Christian, but she must have sensed that I was getting "close."

I went back into aviation, and on a business trip to San Francisco I "got there." I knew I needed help. I was still drinking and smoking incessantly. I was close to being a human wreck. One night there in San Francisco I awoke at 2 o'clock in the morning and broke out in a cold sweat as I sensed that I was a spiritually lost man. I knew that I needed God. I had looked everywhere for the truth but one place, the Bible.

Desperate, I got up and dressed and drove to an all-night department store and searched until I found a Bible. I was the third guy in the checkout line. The first man had a bottle of booze; the second man carried a package of rolls and a paper. The man behind me had a whip! The checkout clerk looked at me and must have thought I was "strange"—who on earth would be buying a Bible at 3 o'clock in the morning!

On my way back to my hotel, I almost wrecked my car as I tried to read the Bible. I was hungry; I had to find the truth, the truth that had been hidden from me for 33 years. In those early morning hours God touched my life as I read the Gospel of Luke, the same man I had read about, "the dear and glorious physician" of the book by that name. I had finally discovered the truth. And the truth was that I was a sinner separated from God—and that Jesus Christ was not a politician who had tried to get together a handful of Jewish revolutionaries 2,000 years ago—but rather He was already a King who had come down from His throne in heaven to shed His blood and suffer and die, so that the sins of Bill Murray could be washed away! So that all could come to know the Father in heaven! And when I realized that, I knew that this was something I could believe *on* and not in; and I got down on my knees and repented of my sins and turned my life over to Jesus Christ, and accepted Him into my heart as Lord and Saviour.

Later I went to one of those "weird" churches where they believe that the Bible is true, and there, as I turned my face to the Lord, I told Him about my problem of drink and tobacco. "Please remove these things from me in the name of Your Son, Jesus," I prayed. And God did. Though I was a chain-smoker, I have not had the desire to smoke since. All things are possible in His name! I discovered that the miracles that change and heal people are available today!

Currently I am still employed in the aviation field as a consultant. I spend much of my time traveling about the country to tell people about the Lord, representing the William J. Murray Faith Foundation. I am working to bring prayer and Bible reading back into public schools. I owe it not only to God but to the nation that my mother and I have damaged.

What is my attitude toward my mother today? Though she thinks I'm crazy and refuses to speak to me, I pray for her. I love her; she's my mother. I feel that she is a 63-year-old, white-haired lady who needs Jesus, and the best thing I can do is pray for her.

I thank the living God, I am no longer an atheist but now love the God my mother taught me to hate!

For a complete account of William J. Murray's story, read his book, *My Life Without God,* published in June 1982 by Thomas Nelson. Bill Murray may be contacted at the William J. Murray Faith Foundation, Inc., 17625 El Camino Real, Suite 405, Houston, Texas 77058. Ask about his testimony on cassette tape.

Darkness vs. Light

Atheism Says:

"Atheism is a natural and inseparable part of Marxism." (V.I. Lenin, *Religion*)

"The most important of more recent events—that 'god is dead,' that the belief in the Christian God has become unworthy of belief—already begins to cast its first shadows over Europe . . . . We philosophers and 'free spirits' feel ourselves irradiated as by a new dawn by the report that the 'old God is dead'; our hearts overflow with gratitude, astonishment, presentiment, and expectation." (Friedrich Nietzsche, *The Joyful Wisdom*)

"Religion is the sigh of the oppressed creature, the sentiment of a heartless world, and the soul of the soulless conditions. It is the opiate of the people. The abolition of religion, as the illusory happiness of men, is a demand for their real happiness." (Karl Marx, *Economics and Philosophical Manuscripts*)

"I believe that when I die I shall rot, and nothing of my ego will survive." (Bertrand Russell, *What I Believe*)

The Bible Says:

"The fool has said in his heart, 'There is no God.' " (David, *Psalm* 53:1)

"See to it that no one takes you captive through philosophy and empty deception, according to the tradition of men." / "Satan disguises himself as an angel of light. Therefore it is not surprising if his servants also disguise themselves as servants of righteousness; whose end shall be according to their deeds." (Apostle Paul, *Colossians* 2:8; *2 Corinthians* 11:14-15)

"The Spirit of the Lord is upon Me, because He anointed Me to preach the Gospel to the poor. He has sent Me to proclaim release to the captives and recovery of sight to the blind, to set free those who are downtrodden, to proclaim the favorable year of the Lord." (Jesus, *Luke* 4:18)

"Those who sleep in the dust of the ground will awake, these to everlasting life, but the others to disgrace and everlasting contempt." (Prophet Daniel, *Daniel* 12:2)

17
Satan Shackled My Soul

by Marie Moore*
as told to Shirley Pope Waite

As I lay in the sleeping bag on the floor of the strange bedroom in Berkeley, California I listened to the steady breathing of Sandy and Chris, my two new friends.

What had happened to me? Three days before, I was a frightened, crazed animal running for my life. Though my body still throbbed with pain from recent beatings, tonight—August 10, 1975—I was experiencing a peace I'd never known before. I tried to understand it all. *Is this for real, or will I wake up in the morning full of hate and revenge again?*

I stiffened. A chill passed through my body as I heard morbid music. From somewhere behind me, I sensed the approach of an evil presence. Satan had come back to claim his own. Panic gripped as I felt pressure on my chest. "I don't belong to you anymore, Satan!"

I tried to call to the girls. My lips were moving, but no sound came. I heard Satan's voice instructing me to give myself totally to him. I was sinking into a trance as I felt his power surge through me. I cried out in my heart to the One I'd met that week.

---

*Real names are not used in this true story. **Shirley Pope Waite** is a homemaker and free-lance writer who resides in Walla Walla, Washington.

"Jesus, please help me! I don't want my old life anymore!" Miraculously, I felt Satan flee, and peace returned.

I guess I'd been easy prey for the evil one since early adolescence. Always a loner, I'd been a heavy drug user from junior high days. During high school, I practiced mental exercises, and in one horrifying LSD trip in 1969, I met Satan for the first time. He actually called me by name!

From that point on, I sought out the spirit world. I never became involved in the satanic cults, but I read the satanic bible faithfully, and got into Tarot cards, palmistry, and TM (Transcendental Meditation).

As my knowledge of the occult world increased, I discovered I had one of Satan's special gifts—the "evil eye"—and with it could exert tremendous power to manipulate others.

I used my "gift" one day on my mother, as she stood pointing a gun at me and screaming, "I should have done this long ago, you no-good . . . !" She often "talked" to me with a revolver in her hand since I had once told her I wanted to kill her. But this time she wilted under my gaze.

I also used the "evil eye" on men to get what I wanted, all the while seeking to satisfy my deep longing for love and acceptance.

This hunger I felt inside was partly satisfied when I met Ernie Moore in 1973. He had just been released from prison and was as lonely and in need of love as I was. We went to Canada for two months, and I came as close to happiness as ever in my 23 years.

Later, Ernie was arrested for parole violation and returned to prison—the Monroe (Washington) Reformatory. The prison chaplain married us in a visiting room within the confines of those walls on August 30, 1974. I wanted to remain true to Ernie, but in my utter loneliness I turned to other men, and I began to study witchcraft seriously.

When Ernie was released, our closeness was gone. A merry-go-round of drugs, guns, satanic worship, and physical violence became our pattern.

Things came to a head in July 1975 when I realized that a covenant had been made with a witch for me to be used as a human sacrifice (animals were usually used, but occasionally a woman was offered). Ernie was to be the mediator. I was terrified. Then one night before the sacrifice was to take place, when he was high on drugs, Ernie beat me viciously, leaving me with a concussion and bruises from head to toe.

I cried out, "God, help me!" Ernie drew back, confused. I was confused too—I'd never used God's name except as a curse. The next day I fled to California, with nothing but the clothes I wore.

After my arrival in Berkeley, my injuries put me in the hospital for two days. When I was released, I thought, *I must get a gun to protect myself.* I headed for San Francisco, where I had heard guns were easy to obtain. The physical pain was nothing compared to the pain of Ernie's hatred. As I walked across the Berkeley campus, I noticed two young women sitting on the grass talking and laughing. They looked so happy. Brazenly, I approached them and asked, "Could you drive me to San Francisco?"

"Why, of course," one said. "But first, how about a meal? You look like you could use one." I wonder now how they had the courage to take me in. I was a mess—dirty, disheveled, gaunt from malnutrition, my face and arms covered with cuts and bruises.

At the dinner table in their apartment, Sandy and Chris made a real effort to be friendly. When they asked questions, I decided to shock them by being totally honest. The shock was mine! They showed concern for me and began to tell me about Jesus Christ.

I wanted to get out of there, but couldn't move! I lit a cigarette. Close to tears, I became increasingly uncomfortable. In the midst of their love, I met the real Marie for the first time. The air was "heavy" as I faced up to the lies, lust, and violence that made up my life. Words thundered through my mind. "Choose now—good or evil—life or death!"

I felt trapped! Then a familiar voice became stronger, "Go get the gun, Marie. Ernie will kill you. I told him where you are. Go get the gun!" I began to scream. Convulsions shook my body. About that time, a young man entered the room and immediately sensed what was happening. I didn't know until later that he was Sandy's fiancé, and had himself been delivered from satanism. He grabbed a Bible and sat across from me, reading Scripture after Scripture. Waves of nausea engulfed me. Perspiring profusely, I moaned and groaned as I felt my body was being torn apart.

"Repeat after me, Marie. 'Jesus, I am a sinner.' "

Pause.

"Jesus—I—am—a—sinner," I croaked. My mouth felt stuffed with cotton balls.

We continued, phrase by phrase: "My life is one of death—

please forgive my sins—come into my heart, Jesus, and make me whole. Let me live, Jesus, and guide my life. . . ."

How long I remained in that semiconscious state, repeating Bible verses and fighting the greatest battle of my life, I do not know. Mere words cannot describe the relief I felt then—the light airy feeling of floating—the sense of love and beauty which surged through every cell of my body. I opened my eyes. Sandy gasped, "Why, you're beautiful, Marie!" I was brand new!

After Satan's unsuccessful attempt to lure me back that night in the bedroom, I knew Christ had won the victory. My hatred gone, I wanted to contact Ernie and share my newfound faith with him. He had been searching in five states for me, breathing threats and curses.

I wish I could have seen his face when he received my letter. It couldn't have been any greater shock for him than when he actually saw me. When I opened the door of the youth center where I'd been staying, and where I'd arranged to meet him, he walked right past me. My own husband didn't recognize me!

Christ has since become a reality for Ernie, but not until after he got into real trouble again.

As I write this, he is out on parole after serving time in the state penitentiary. We are separated as Ernie attempts to piece his life together. I pray that he too will learn to rely totally on Jesus as I have done.

It grieves me to hear people laugh and joke about Satan's reality. They don't realize his power, cunning, and subtlety. But I praise God "because greater is He who is in . . . [me] than he who is in the world" (1 John 4:4). Christ entered into my hell and brought me into His precious light—and I am no longer a daughter of darkness!

Darkness vs. Light

Satanism Says:
"The true image of the Satanist, from the beginning of what, by one name or another, would be considered Satanism, is that of the Master, the Leader, the controller of societies, the image makers. All these people that have been winners have practiced intrinsically a Satanic concept of life." (Anton LaVey, "The Church of Satan," *McCalls*, March 1970)

"According to one powerful faction of the spiritual underground . . . the whispering serpent only wanted to regain title to paradise. For the snake stands for . . . nature and wisdom and peace—without God—and people want these things badly." (Colin Campbell, "Who Really Owned Eden?" *Psychology Today*, December 1975)

"My church is based on indulgence. Eventually I want to build pleasure domes—retreats for my followers. . . . We believe in the pleasures of the flesh, living to the hilt, enjoying all there is to be on earth." (Anton LaVey, in *The Truth About Witchcraft*, by Hanz Holzer)

The Bible Says:
"You [Lucifer] said in your heart, 'I will ascend to heaven; I will raise my throne above the stars of God. . . . I will make myself like the Most High. Nevertheless you will be thrust down to Sheol, to the recesses of the pit." (Prophet Isaiah, *Isaiah* 14:13-15)

"[The devil] does not stand in the truth, because there is no truth in him . . . he is a liar, and the father of lies." (Jesus, *John* 8:44) / "And he [an angel] laid hold of the dragon, the serpent of old, who is the Devil and Satan . . . and threw him into the abyss . . . that he should not deceive the nations any longer." (Apostle John, *Revelation* 20:2-3)

"We too all formerly lived in the lusts of our flesh, indulging the desires of the flesh and of the mind, and were by nature children of wrath, even as the rest. But God, being rich in mercy, because of His great love with which He loved us, even when we were dead in our transgressions, made us alive together with Christ." (Apostle Paul, *Ephesians* 2:3-5)

18
Hedonism Put Me behind Bars

*by Gwynn Lewis
as told to Steve Lawhead*

As a high school guy in Ohio, I couldn't wait to get out and see the world. I saw my parents working every day, year after year. For what? I certainly couldn't tell. And the only thing I knew for sure was that I didn't want to end up slaving my life away, as they were.

I promised myself that as soon as I graduated I was going to see it all. Travel. Adventure. I didn't have money, but I didn't need any either. I'd heard of friends making it all the way to New York hitching on a single ride. That's what I would do.

Rock concerts and dope are what I remember of New York and the big-city life. First I was introduced to the dope scene, then came three hectic years of college and running from Uncle Sam, trying to stay out of Vietnam. I ran to the West Coast, the hip place to be.

San Francisco turned ugly not long after I got there. It was Haight-Ashbury, flower power, free love, and psychedelics. The migration of the long-haired herds had just begun. It was going to be a paradise on earth; we'd show the uptight world how life

---

Gwynn Lewis is a 1980 graduate of North Park Theological Seminary, Chicago and now is a missionary in Costa Rica, with his wife. *Steve Lawhead* formerly served on the editorial staff of *Campus Life* magazine. He now lives in Memphis and works fulltime as a free-lance writer.

should be lived. We'd create a mighty love force that would sweep the continent. We'd bring the establishment to its knees—with love.

But the beautiful dream of universal peace and love dissolved in the smoke of water pipes and LSD crystals. What started out as a quaint community of free spirits deteriorated into a garish slum. The place was a sewer when I left.

Somewhere along Route 66 in New Mexico a state patrol car stopped me. I had long hair, and policemen were wary of longhairs in those days. The word was out—all longhairs were hippies, dopeheads with Communist tendencies. They hauled me out of the car and proceeded to tear everything apart, looking for grass. They found two joints, and I was off to jail. A few months later, in an open-and-shut case, I was sentenced to 10 years in the state penitentiary.

I had served 18 months of my sentence when my case came up for a review. The state supreme court decided they'd been a little harsh on me, so I was given a new trial, sentenced to two years and immediately given a year's parole. When I finished that, the judge tacked on another year of parole. I turned my minibus around, jumped parole, and headed for L.A.

Back in California I drifted around, settling for a while in Berkeley. I was still into dope pretty heavily, and I still believed in the peace-love movement. Maybe we'd gone about it the wrong way, I thought. I met a girl named Pooka and we started hanging around together, then living together.

Dope is an expensive habit. If you don't have a job to support it, or the nerves for stealing, you get pretty desperate. I cooked up a great way to beat the high cost of "flying." *In South America where the dope grows wild,* I reasoned, *I can keep myself in dope by hardly lifting a finger. I can live for peanuts down there.* Pooka agreed to come along, and once again I was on the road.

Quito, Ecuador is about as far away from Ohio as a person can get in terms of culture and lifestyle. It was pure adventure. I felt as if I had arrived.

I scouted around for a place to live and found a little farm planted in the foothills of the mountains a few miles out of Quito. There Pooka and I settled down to the "good life" of cheap dope and no hassles.

I busied myself collecting pre-Columbian artifacts, pottery, and gold for export to the States. The natives made the most exquisite woolen sweaters, so I went into partnership with a man from Seattle to export them. I'd buy them until I had a shipment of around 200, which I'd bundle and send off to him. I would make $4000 for my part of the deal, a small fortune down there.

In the meantime, I was making trips up the mountain to where the natives, untouched by law and order or civilization, cultivated coca plants. I'd buy coca leaves in small quantities, just enough for myself and my friends. Back home I'd treat the leaves with chemicals I kept on hand to make cocaine. It was a slick setup, and I thought I was living like a king.

Then one night the sky fell in on my paradise. Two cars pulled into the yard and men in suits piled out and surrounded the house. "It's the police!" I screamed, running through the house. "Get rid of everything!"

I went out into the yard to talk to them, pretending I didn't understand their Spanish. They shoved me aside and with their guns out busted into the house. Once inside, the police, from Interpol, the international police organization, started pulling everything apart. They went through the house with the mindless precision of a junk shredder.

The search and seizure was complete, but failed to turn up any evidence of the kind they were looking for. Apparently, the small amount of dope I had on hand wasn't what they were after. The police-machine, however, didn't give up and continued the search until one of them found the cache of chemicals I used for processing the coke leaves. That was it, evidence made to order. They rounded up the chemicals, handcuffed me, snatched our baby out of the crib, and stuffed Pooka, the baby, and me into a car.

We arrived at the police headquarters in Quito about 3 A.M. They separated Pooka and me and left me alone to contemplate my fate.

I didn't have very long to think. Three men came and led me upstairs to the interrogation room. In the middle of the floor was a tree stump. I couldn't understand the barrage of questions in Spanish, and I fumbled for words. Suddenly the smallest of the three men unleashed a karate punch, and I found myself on the floor gasping for air.

They stood me up and took off my clothes. Completely naked, I shivered. My hands were thrust behind my back and my thumbs were laced together with my own shoelaces. Then they tied another rope between my thumbs. They propped me up on the stump, and looped the rope over the center beam of the ceiling, pulling it tight and tying it to a hook on the wall. I stood on the stump, dangling on tiptoes, my arms stretched out behind me, pulled taut by the rope. Then one of the men kicked the stump out from under me.

The pain was terrible. As I swung in the air before their eyes, they asked more questions. How long had I been smuggling? How much? What were my connections? When I didn't answer with the kind of answer they wanted, or even if I did, one of the men whacked me with a heavy board. In about two minutes I blacked out.

They took me down and dumped me in a cell. Actually, it was a large, rectangular room underground. There was no water. No toilet. No bunks or benches. It contained 60 or 70 men, crammed together in the dark. The only light came from a naked light bulb hanging by a wire. We used one corner for a latrine and slept on the other side of the room. Once a day they came and hosed down the room and evenings about 6 o'clock we were allowed to receive any food that might have been brought to us. The prison served no food—we had to arrange for someone to bring food from the outside.

The next day they again took me to the interrogation room and hung me up by my thumbs, which were sore from the first round of torture. The experience was more painful the second time. The police wanted me to sign a paper confessing to every unsolved dope-related crime they had on their books. Again I refused.

The third day, my swollen, purple thumbs throbbed when I moved my hands. I agreed to sign the confession, but they tied me up anyway and swung me one last time, smashing that board against my spine, to punish me for what I had done.

Word got around that I was in prison. Some people I knew showed up with food one night and agreed to bring more. I still hadn't seen Pooka to know how she was. I worried about her and the baby, but my friends said they had brought some food for her too and they would see that she got it.

About the third week, Pooka was released. The authorities had decided to deport her rather than keep her in jail with a baby. She snatched a few minutes to tell me good-bye and give me her blanket. She said she'd come back if she could. Then she was whisked away, under armed guard to the Colombian border and released. I didn't know if I'd ever see her again.

Days drifted into one another. Weeks passed, days of mental anguish, weeks of doubt and frustration. Two things happened to improve my situation somewhat. I was moved from the underground prison to one above ground. It had windows and wooden-frame beds lined up in rows with an aisle down the middle like a hospital room.

My fellow convicts, 11 in all, weren't desperados or banditos, but more what you'd call "white collar" criminals. There was an engineer who'd built a bridge that collapsed and killed some people, a lawyer who'd been accused of shifty dealings, and so on.

The other thing that helped me to keep my sanity was Pooka's return. She had sneaked back into the country with the baby. After arriving in Colombia, she put her passport into the wash with her laundry. The passport was ruined. The punched holes on the passport cover were all she needed to have a new one issued. She waited a few weeks for the new one and then came back across the border to Quito to try to help me get out.

One day an American businessman arrived in Quito looking for someone to work with on a dope deal. In the States he had financial backers who wanted to smuggle marijuana and cocaine from South America for resale in the States. Someone gave him my name, since I was supposed to be a notorious dope smuggler. He got in touch with Pooka and she relayed the message to me: $1,000 for setting up the connections. I knew where the connections were to be made all right, but Pooka would have to do it. Ordinarily I wouldn't have touched the deal, or put Pooka in a position like that.

The risk was high, but the return was higher. A thousand dollars was a fortune. Pooka and the baby were starving in a sleazy hotel room a couple blocks from the prison. We had no money for food, let alone to pay off the lawyers to work on my case. The money would go a long way toward solving our problems. In the end I left it up to Pooka.

She said yes. The American applied pressure to make sure things went his way. Plans proceeded.

About this time, my mother, thousands of miles away in

Chicago, got in touch with a missionary. He was a young guy visiting the States before heading back to Ecuador. She asked him to visit me in prison and gave him $25 for me. His name was Jerry Reed, and he started visiting me as soon as he got back.

I wasn't even slightly interested in religion, but I was glad to see a friendly face. Jerry didn't try to push Jesus on me; he was interested in helping me and being my friend. He gave me some books to read and told me he'd look out for Pooka and our baby.

The date for the connection deal was set. Pooka was very nervous about the whole thing, but the money was so important to us she was afraid to back out. She was afraid of the American businessman too. He was deadly serious; there was no telling what he would do if he got mad.

Then something strange happened. The day before the deal was to take place, Pooka was lying on her bed in her hotel room when she heard a voice. She looked around, but she knew she was alone. The voice said, "I know you and all your problems. You don't have to do this deal. We'll work it out."

Instantly, she knew the voice of Jesus had spoken to her. "All right, Lord, You're on!" she said. From that moment she believed everything would be all right. She knelt down and prayed for a long time. In that hotel room at that moment, she accepted Christ and became a Christian. She prayed that the same thing would happen to me.

The next day Pooka got up and went to the American and told him the deal was off. He looked at her in surprise—I guess because he knew how much we needed the money, and he figured we couldn't back out. But all he said was, "OK."

I knew nothing about all of this. I was sitting in my cell waiting for something to happen. I'd been reading the Bible—one of the books Jerry had given me. I didn't think it would have any effect on me; it was a way to pass the time. But it started me thinking. *Here I am locked up in jail, and who knows when I'll get out. My girlfriend and child are starving in a cheap hotel room because of me, and there's nothing I can do about it. . . .* I was totally at the mercy of things I couldn't control.

Well, there was *one* thing I hadn't tried, I thought as I sat looking at the Bible. I hadn't tried Christ. Even as I pondered, it seemed right. There weren't any doubts—and I'd always had doubts before.

As I sat there thinking quite rationally and logically, I knew God would help me. I also knew that if I became a Christian, it would have to be 100 percent.

In a few moments I made up my mind to receive Christ and to try His way. I felt it was the right decision, but I worried about what Pooka would think. I didn't have the courage to tell her myself, so I wrote a note to give her when she came with my food that night. I wrote, "Dear Pooka, this is going to blow your mind. I've decided to become a Christian."

About 6 P.M. I left the cell and went out into the courtyard and on to the gate. Pooka and Jerry were there. She told me the drug deal was off. At that point I didn't really care. I slipped her the note and took my food and left.

Within 24 hours Pooka and I had become Christians. It was totally unbelievable. I didn't know what to do next—what was a Christian supposed to do? When Jerry visited me later, I asked him what I should do. He showed me which books of the Bible to start reading, and right away I began learning about Jesus. The more I read, the more I was certain Christ was the author of my unusual experience. I had met Him personally and felt His presence there with me in prison.

When a person becomes a Christian, you hear all kinds of stories of how everything changes radically for the better. Not so with me. I was happier and more confident than ever before that I would get out, but circumstances remained much the same. Pooka and Jerry kept working, trying to keep my lawyer honest, trying to convince a judge to look at my case—begging, pleading with anyone in authority who would listen.

Jerry said that his church back in the States was praying for me. I thought about that for a long time: people I didn't even know, who'd never met me, were praying for *me,* a jailbird in a foreign country!

The three of us decided Easter would be a fine, symbolic time for me to be released, so we started praying that I would be freed on or before Easter. The police wanted a 12-year conviction (16 years was a maximum life sentence). The judge was leaning toward a 6-year sentence, but he kept postponing his decision, promising to deliver a verdict the next week, and on and on.

Month by month Easter drew closer. Then one day, a week before Easter, the judge decided to review the evidence relating to my case. The police brought him a box of confiscated articles they had taken from my house—evidence like the drug-processing chemicals, bags of cocaine, and other incriminating items.

The judge put the box on his desk and opened it. Peering inside, he found a few empty plastic bottles, nothing else. All the evidence had vanished. The chemicals had evaporated, and the police had pilfered the rest. In effect, they had nothing on me. The judge took one look and said, "I'm not going to convict a man with this kind of evidence—empty bottles." He ordered my release.

It was late afternoon before Pooka and Jerry were able to complete all the necessary papers. But they obtained my "ticket," a signed order for my release, and made a mad dash for the prison. They arrived at precisely 4:55—only five minutes before the gates would close for Easter holidays. I was free at last! The ordeal was over.

The very next day Pooka and I stood before Jerry, and he officially married us. The following week we flew back to the States to meet the people of Jerry's church who had been praying for us for so long, to thank them for all they had done for us. It was a fantastic reunion.

Since I became a Christian, my new life has so overshadowed the old one, I find it hard to understand how I did the things I did. I was a hedonist living strictly for self, for the pleasure I could get out of life. It seems to me now that the whole adventure happened to someone else, and, in a sense it did. I am no longer the person I was. God has seen to that.

Darkness vs. Light

Hedonism Says:

"How is it possible to conceive of good, except in terms of taste, of sound, of sight, and of sexual pleasure? The beginning and root of all good reside in the belly, even wisdom and the enjoyments of a cultivated mind derive from these." (Epicurus, in *On The Nature Of Things,* by Lucretius)

"We must not be afraid or ashamed of sex; sex is not necessarily limited to marriage; sex is oxygen, mental health. Enough of virginity, hypocrisy, censorship, restrictions. Pleasure is to be preferred to sorrow." (Hugh Hefner, quoted by Oriana Fallaci, *Look* magazine, March 10, 1967)

"I've never called him Dad or Daddy, because he's not exactly the Dad or Daddy type." (Christie Hefner, "This is Hugh Hefner's Daughter," *Esquire,* December 1973)

"A girl or boy should be free to have a sex life when she or he wants it. Without parental approval, such a sex life would be apt to be a guilty one; without contraceptives, a dangerous one." (A.S. Neill, *Freedom—Not License!)*

The Bible Says:

"I collected for myself silver and gold, and the treasure of kings and provinces." / "And all that my eyes desired I did not refuse them. I did not withhold my heart from any pleasure. ... Thus I considered all my activities ... and behold all was vanity and striving after wind and there was no profit under the sun." (Solomon, *Ecclesiastes* 2:8, 10-11)

"Many will follow their sensuality and because of them the way of the truth will be maligned." (Apostle Peter, *2 Peter* 2:2) / "Flee immorality. Every other sin that a man commits is outside the body, but the immoral man sins against his own body." (Apostle Paul, *1 Corinthians* 6:18)

"Fathers, do not exasperate your children, that they may not lose heart." (Apostle Paul, *Colossians* 3:21)

"Flee from youthful lusts, and pursue righteousness, faith, love, and peace, with those who call on the Lord from a pure heart." (Apostle Paul, *2 Timothy* 2:22)

SECTION 4
The Trip Out

19
Clues to the Cults
by Dave Breese

Each cult is guilty of one or more doctrinal errors. Once you know what these typical errors are, you can know what's basically wrong with a cult, whatever weird or seemingly rational form it may take. Awareness of these characteristics can help you spot creeping errors among true Christians too and maybe save you from going astray.

This chapter will help you determine where any given cult is in error. The material has been adapted from Dave Breese's helpful book *Know the Marks of Cults* © 1975 by SP Publications and published by Victor Books. The author travels widely as a speaker, ministering as president of Christian Destiny, Inc., Hillsboro, Kansas.

---

*All Scripture quotations in "Clues to the Cults" are from the *King James Version*.

1/Extra-biblical Revelation

Hebrews 1:1-2* makes it perfectly clear: "God, who at sundry times and in diverse manners spoke in time past unto the fathers by the prophets, hath in these last days spoken unto us by His Son."

A cardinal doctrine of Christianity is that final truth, the ultimate Word, is resident in Jesus Christ. Indeed the Scripture is even stronger than that, saying, "In the beginning was the Word, and the Word was with God, and the Word was God" (John 1:1).

Final truth, therefore, is the Person, the Word, and the work of Jesus Christ. No subsequent revelation can supersede the revelation of Jesus Christ.

The most typical characteristic of a cult is that it claims for its authority some revelation apart from the clear statement of the Word of God. Most cults claim to respect the Bible, but then quickly announce confidence in some subsequent revelation that in effect cancels the teaching of the Bible. Sometimes this extra-biblical revelation comes in the form of a "divinely inspired leader."

2/A False Basis of Salvation

The clear teaching of the New Testament is that eternal salvation comes to a believer solely as a result of faith in Jesus Christ. The New Testament Scriptures declare again and again this sublime Christian truth: "Therefore being justified by faith, we have peace with God through our Lord Jesus Christ" (Romans 5:1). / "For by grace are ye saved through faith; and that not of yourselves; it is the gift of God, not of works, lest any man should boast" (Ephesians 2:8-9).

These and many other clear declarations of the New Testament positively establish the basis of salvation to be the finished work of Christ alone and our faith in that work.

By contrast, Scripture teaches that attempts at salvation, based on human efforts, are cursed by God. "For as many as are of the works of the Law are under the curse; for it is written, 'Cursed is everyone that continueth not in all things which are written in the book of the Law to do them.' But that no man is justified by the Law in the sight of God, it is evident: for, 'The just shall live by faith'" (Galatians 3:10-11).

Every cult in the world preaches "another gospel" and will lead finally to human despair, death, and hell. Millions could be saved from this spiritual tragedy if they would respond to the promise of Scripture, "Believe on the Lord Jesus Christ, and thou shalt be saved" (Acts 16:31).

3/Uncertain Hope

We shouldn't be surprised that a nearly universal characteristic of cults is insistence that one can not be sure of eternal life while in this world. The issue of salvation is never settled. The follower lives in constant fear that he has not done enough, given enough, prayed enough, or worshiped enough to be sure of salvation.

In view of this, one suspects that the cults are really not talking about salvation at all, but rather are pushing religious philosophies tied to a set of unrealizable goals in the name of which they can extract every kind of sacrifice from their hapless followers.

A common characteristic of cults is that they are devoid of a theological structure that offers to anyone a sure salvation. It would be unthinkable for a cultist ever to say in the words of Scripture, "For I am persuaded, that neither death, nor life, nor angels, nor principalities, nor powers, nor things present, nor things to come, nor height, nor depth, nor any other creature, shall be able to separate us from the love of God, which is in Christ Jesus our Lord" (Romans 8:38-39).

In contrast to cultic fear, a Christian can say in the words of the Apostle Paul, "I know whom I have believed, and am persuaded that He is able to keep that which I have committed unto Him against that day" (2 Timothy 1:12).

4/Presumptuous Messianic Leadership

One of the marks of a cult is that it elevates the person and the words of a human leader to a messianic level. The predictable characteristic of a cult member is that he will soon be quoting his leader, whether Father Divine, Prophet Jones, Mary Baker Eddy, Judge Rutherford, or Herbert Armstrong, as a final authority. A messianic human leader has used the powers of his intelligence or personality and with them imposed his ideas and directives on the ignorant.

The Christian message is that Jesus Christ is the Author and Finisher of our faith (Hebrews 12:2). He alone is our High Priest (Hebrews 4:14). He alone is our Mediator (1 Timothy 2:5). The church is the body of Christ, of which He is the head (Ephesians 1:22-23).

Only Jesus Christ deserves disciples.

5/Doctrinal Ambiguity

Doctrinal ambiguity is a mark of a cult. One of the fascinating characteristics of the cults is the interesting and sometimes hilarious changes of doctrine through which they pass. Doctrines are being continually altered in order to adapt to new situations, arguments, or the whims of their leaders. They know nothing of the command of Scripture, "That we henceforth be no more children, tossed to and fro, and carried about with every wind of doctrine, by the sleight of men, and cunning craftiness, . . . to deceive" (Ephesians 4:14). Scripture is clear that craftily changing doctrine is a cunning device used by those who prey upon the unwary.

The illustrations are many. During and after the days of Mary Baker Eddy, the Christian Science cult republished her book *Science and Health with Key to the Scriptures* nearly every year. The annual update made it possible for the contradictions and doctrines of the past to be adapted to the demands of the present.

The Word of God clearly warns that "the time will come when they will not endure sound doctrine; but after their own lusts shall they heap to themselves teachers, having itching ears; and they shall turn away their ears from the truth, and shall be turned into fables" (2 Timothy 4:3-4).

6/The Claim of "Special Discoveries"

One is amazed to see the large and loyal following that comes to people who report some vision, presence, revelation, or special discovery which has come to them and which they claim to be divine. It would be impossible to have a cult without mysterious, otherwise unavailable inside information. In one way or another, each of these religions traffics in such hallucinations.

No discovery in the entire universe is superior to the discovery of salvation in Jesus Christ. There is no higher information, no better revelation, no deeper truth—nothing is greater than the knowledge of Christ. The person who turns from this greatest discovery, this ultimate revelation, to pursue the delusions of a cult leader is a fool. Despite this obvious truth, the cults continue to beguile unstable souls with false claims to special discoveries. No discovery is more special than Jesus Christ.

Nearly all cult leaders boast of a purported revelation. These persons claim divine authority for a private, unauthenticated religious event. They claim to have seen a vision of a woman on a mountain, heard a voice in a prayer tower, or been visited by an angel who came with golden tablets and giant spectacles. The unsubstantiated and largely preposterous stories are endless.

7/Defective Christology

In the history of the church, the most grievous heresies have been those which have advocated a view of the person of Christ other than that which is taught in the Word of God. Satan knows that an improper understanding of the person and the work of Christ makes salvation impossible.

The historical precedent of cultic attacks on the person of Christ should lead us not to be surprised at cultic detractions today. *Most cults active in our time deny the true deity of Christ, the true humanity of Jesus, or the true union of the two natures in one Person.*

The question, "What think ye of Jesus?" is answered correctly only by the believing Christian. Only he can say: "Jesus Christ is the only begotten Son of the living God, God incarnate in the form of human flesh. He is the Son of man, the only Saviour of the world, the Author and Finisher of faith, who, through His death on the cross, provides redemption for all who believe in Him. He died for our sins, rose again on the third day, and lives to make intercession for us before His Father. He will one day come in His glorious returning to judge the quick and the dead at His appearing in His kingdom. He is Lord and God, and in Him alone we have life, and life more abundantly."

Closely related to the fatal heresy of defective Christology is a denial of the trinity of the Godhead. The only true God is one

God, eternally existent in three persons, Father, Son, and Holy Spirit. Each person of the Godhead is coequal and coeternal with the others.

8/Segmented Biblical Attention

The temptation of groups of serious conviction is to move ever further from the central pale of reason that C.S. Lewis calls "mere Christianity." Because of their emphasis, they begin declaring that "love is everything," or "history is all-important." They take some important, but not critical emphasis of Scripture, and move it to the exalted position of an imperative doctrine. They move their test of fellowship away from Jesus Christ to some lesser point.

It is a grave temptation for any group to find a verse in the Bible about holiness, the kingdom, law, grace, works, faith, or something else and use it as a substitute for a whole counsel of God. Even zealous Christians frequently have fallen into the trap of segmented biblical interpretation, thereby creating a cultic influence in their system of doctrine.

Christian maturity will save us from all of this.

9/Enslaving Organizational Structure

The promoters of the cults obey no such rules as Scripture lays down for leaders. Indeed, they know that their success is directly dependent on their ability to trap followers into a permanent entanglement. Association is almost invariably formed with the bonds of fear. The leader's preaching, teaching, and efforts are dedicated not to producing individual competence and freedom on the part of his followers, but to creating dependence. The leaders of the cults work to promote slavery, not liberty.

To them the purpose of a religious organization is not that it becomes a living segment of the body of Christ, but rather a personally exploitable syndicate. It is a monolithic, merciless, and entangling organizational structure.

A cultic leader may present his wares by saying, "Come to Jesus," but his real theme song is "You Belong to Me." The Christian is well advised to heed the advice of the Apostle Paul: "Stand fast therefore in the liberty wherewith Christ hath made us free, and be not entangled again with the yoke of bondage" (Galatians 5:1).

The only *imperative* membership which the true Christian recognizes is in the body of Christ. He may belong to a group which emphasizes membership in the local church, but he places no confidence in this as the *basis for his eternal life*. The perceptive Christian is a unique kind of an individual in that he is unable to be "organized" in the same sense as others who place life-and-death importance on their organizational involvement. Jesus Christ has set him free, and no one is entitled to take this freedom from him.

10/Financial Exploitation

It is clear from the Word of God that the Christian is never put under obligation to do, give, sacrifice, or expend himself in any way in order to be more sure that he has the gift of God which is eternal life. He is invited in many earnest ways to commit himself to the service of Christ and to become a useful instrument in the hands of God. The Word of God, however, is clear that serving Christ is a voluntary proposition on the part of the Christian, and nothing that he does will increase his guarantee of eternal life. He is saved by grace and kept by the power of God. His eternal life came to him without payment on his part. It is dependent wholly on the work of Christ on the cross.

In contrast the cultic practitioner of today strongly implies that money contributed to the cause will buy privileges, gifts, or powers for the follower. He offers healing for $100. He offers deliverance from accident for life for $1,000. The follower of the cult is often promised that he can escape the many purgatories in this world and the next through the investment of his money.

In the financial structure of the average cult, tithing is but the beginning. Then comes the real pressure. As the screw is turned, the follower is exploited to the point of economic exhaustion.

11/Denunciation of Others

When one announces himself as the true "messiah," all others, of course, are false and must be put down. Some of the most bitter imprecations in print are the scathing calumny of cultic messiahs on those who do not believe their views and join their organizations.

One sometimes suspects that these leaders are infected with an inferiority complex, pushing them to a neurotic defensiveness. They are for the most part unwilling to appear in public debate or answer questions concerning the nature of their faith from perceptive Christian scholars. Expressing their persecution complex, they denounce all alternative views as satanic and corrupt.

Much unsettlement has been caused in the ranks of Christians by those with pretended convictions who demand a hearing and who are purveyors of a new discovery of truth. The Apostle Paul earnestly exhorted, "Now I beseech you, brethren, mark them which cause divisions and offenses contrary to the doctrine which ye have learned; and avoid them. For they that are such serve not our Lord Jesus Christ, but their own belly; and by good words and fair speeches deceive the hearts of the simple" (Romans 16:17-18).

12/Syncretism

Syncretism describes the attempt to gather together what some would call "the best qualities" of various religious points of view into a new and acceptable faith. It is the attempt to "synchronize" the otherwise diverse religious elements currently believed by people so as to make a new religion attractive.

Syncretism is a favorite cultic device. Both the older and the emergent cults, almost without exception, have accommodated themselves to existing religious points of view, incorporating older doctrines into their systems of faith along with new and creative heresies. Few cults of our time present much that is really new in the world of religion. Almost invariably they are a rehash of existing concepts, orthodox and heretical. They present warmed-over elements of Protestantism, Catholicism, paganism, pantheism, idolatry, local fetishes, and pure idiocy.

Syncretism, the attempt to synchronize the Gospel of Christ with a godless world, is a deadly virus from which almost no institution recovers. This virus can infect us and, becoming a plague, can carry us away. When the Son of man is come, will He find faith on the earth?

EPILOGUE
God's Way
by Billy Graham

Adolf Eichmann, according to a minister who talked with him before his execution, had a religion. He claimed to believe in a personal God who "did not judge sin" and "would not condemn anyone." The man who exterminated millions of Jews was trying, as others have tried before him, to build his own religion.

There are many religions in the world, but only one Christianity, for only Christianity has a God who gave Himself for mankind. World religions attempt to reach up to God; Christianity is God reaching down to man.

The Bible shows very clearly how God moved through the ages in carrying out His plan to redeem mankind, and the story is told in words short and simple. One of these short and profound words is "made." In accordance with God's eternal purpose, Christ was *made* in the likeness of man so that man might be *made* in the likeness of God—the prince literally taking the place of the pauper in order that the pauper might become a prince.

God's justice required that sin be punished, but His mercy provided a substitute for man in the person of Christ. The Bible teaches that Christ and God are one. In the triune Godhead there

---

Evangelist *Billy Graham* has preached the Gospel over much of the world, and continues to hold citywide crusades in his fourth decade of ministry. His ministry is headquartered in Minneapolis.

is no distinction of substance, only of manifestation. Therefore, in the person of His Son, God Himself suffered the punishment for sin.

First, Christ was *made flesh*. The Bible says, "In the beginning was the Word, and the Word was with God, and the Word was God . . . without Him was not anything made that was made. . . . And the Word was made flesh, and dwelt among us" (John 1:1, 3, 14*). This great miracle through the virgin birth was the result of the greater miracle of God so loving this sinful, warring, wicked world that He gave Himself in the person of Christ for its redemption.

When King Jesus was born in the flesh, it became possible for man to be born of the Holy Spirit. That is the reason Jesus could say, "Ye must be born again" (John 3:7).

A Marxist, speaking in Hyde Park in London some time ago, pointed to a man in rags. He cried, "Communism can put a new suit of clothes on that man." A Christian standing nearby pointed to the man and shouted, "Christ can put a new man in that suit." That is the difference between Communism and Christianity. Christ came in the flesh in order to make new men and women and to make a new society and a new race of men. You are not simply reformed when you come to Christ; He does not just put a new suit on you. Jesus Christ makes you a new person. He gives you a new heart. You are regenerated by the Spirit of God. This is what being born again means.

Second, the Bible teaches that Christ was *made sin*. History records the repeated failure of man to attain righteousness by his own methods. The Old and New Testaments tell us the same story. Man failed in Eden and carried the human race down with him. In the days of Noah, "God looked upon the earth, and behold, it was corrupt; for all flesh had corrupted His way upon the earth" (Genesis 6:11); and God destroyed that generation.

When men multiplied, they sought again to attain heaven by the work of their own hands at Babel. God dispersed them by confusing their language, and that is the reason we have various languages and dialects in the world.

---

*All Scripture quotations in this article are from the *King James Version*.

Today we have the same spectacle that history records time after time—the spectacle of a civilization committing suicide. A continuous record of thousands of years proves that the possibility of arriving at moral perfection by natural evolution is a will o' the wisp. A power greater than man's must intervene for his salvation, and that is what God provides in Christ's act of substitution. "He hath made Him to be sin for us, [Him] who knew no sin; that we might be made the righteousness of God in Him" (2 Corinthians 5:21). Christ took the responsibility for your sins and mine when He died on the cross. More than that, the Scripture says, "The Lord hath laid on Him the iniquity of us all" (Isaiah 53:6). He voluntarily took your sins and mine and was actually counted to be a sinner.

Third, Christ was *made a curse.* Sin is alien to God. Just as righteousness brings blessing, so sin brings a curse. When Christ was crucified, He bore in His body the curse of sin. The cross itself is a symbol of sin—it was for robbers, murderers, and outcasts. The Old Testament Law said, "Cursed is every one that hangeth on a tree" (Deuteronomy 21:23). The Cross is a symbol of that curse, and Christ bore the curse of sin when He died. Therefore it is written that "Christ hath redeemed us from the curse of the Law, being made a curse for us" (Galatians 3:13).

Fourth, Christ was *made poor.* No human imagination can comprehend the infinite riches of Christ in heaven before He became flesh. He was heir of all things, yet as our substitute He was born in a cattle shed, lived with common people, and had no place to lay His head. He lacked even a single coin to pay the Roman tax, and He was buried in a borrowed tomb. He was poor, yet He made many rich; He had nothing, yet He possessed all things. This was a voluntary poverty of One who turned water into wine and fed a multitude with a few loaves and fish. Christ was made poor that you might be made spiritually rich.

Fifth, Christ was *made a servant.* The Scripture says that He "made Himself of no reputation, and took upon Him the form of a servant, and was made in the likeness of men" (Philippians 2:17). He washed the feet of His followers. He humbled Himself in order that He might exalt man to His own royal estate. The Bible also says that Christ "hath made us kings and priests unto God and His Father" (Revelation 1:6). In His voluntary humiliation, Christ was made a servant that every one of us might be made royalty.

Every man and woman who possesses Jesus Christ has royal blood; he has been adopted into the royal family of heaven. It is the family of the redeemed, and all of that family are possessors of life eternal. You may someday be carried to your grave, but there is a resurrection. The Bible says that the same Spirit "that raised up Christ from the dead shall also quicken your mortal bodies" (Romans 8:11). With this resurrection body you can live in the presence of God and with the family of God forever. Death and the grave are no threat to the children of God. On the other side of the grave we will live forever. "There shall be no more death," the Bible says, "neither sorrow, nor crying, neither shall there be any more pain" (Revelation 21:4). All that we now associate with death will be no more—no caskets, no funerals, no crepe on the door, no flags at half-mast. The Bible says, "The former things are passed away" (v. 4).

We are looking forward to the day when we shall rise from the dead. Because Jesus lives, we believers are going to live also. The Gospel is not only the death and burial of Christ—the Gospel includes the resurrection of Christ. Without His resurrection there is no Christianity; it is the crux of Christianity.

Sixth, Christ was *made a reject.* More than 700 years before our Lord came to earth, Isaiah prophesied that the Messiah would be despised and rejected of men. Before His death, Jesus Christ Himself said that He must be rejected by His generation. As our substitute, Christ was rejected of men, that all those who accept Him as Saviour might be accepted of God. There is no possibility that you can know God the Father without first coming into vital contact with Jesus Christ the Son. Jesus said, "I am the way, the truth, and the life: no man cometh unto the Father, but by Me" (John 14:6). Christianity teaches that you cannot know God, you can have no contact with God, unless you come through His Son, Jesus Christ. There is no other way to heaven, no other way of spiritual salvation than through Jesus Christ.

Last, Christ was *made an outcast from God* for us. His suffering on the cross was more than physical; it was the far greater agony of spiritual separation from God. When Jesus cried, "My God, My God, why hast Thou forsaken Me?" He clearly showed that whatever else hell may be, it certainly is separation from God. This was the agony of spirit which forced from Jesus' lips the anguished cry of "forsaken" during the hours of darkness which shrouded the cross. In this separation from God, He reached the depths of His punishment for the sin which separates man from God, and thereby raised the believer to the glory which Christ laid down in his behalf. Therefore it is written that "God, who is rich in mercy, for His great love wherewith He loved us, even when we were dead in sins, hath quickened us together with Christ . . . and hath raised us up together, and made us sit together in heavenly places in Christ Jesus" (Ephesians 2:4, 6).

In God's plan of redemption by substitution, Christ was separated from God that every one of us who believes in Him might know God and one day ascend into heaven.

It is only in Christ's dying on the cross for us that we can see the sinful depths of mankind. You can never understand sin, you can never understand what it means to transgress the Law of God unless you look at the cross. You can see a sinful world about you and you will understand a little of the sinful depths of the human heart. But for true comprehension you must go to the cross of Christ and find the holy Son of God dying there. And the Bible says you are responsible as much as anyone else in the human race for putting Jesus Christ on the cross, because you are a sinner. The Bible says, "All have sinned and come short of the glory of God." The Bible says, "The wages of sin is death." The Bible says, "The soul that sinneth, it shall die." And Jesus Christ bore all your sin.

The cross of Christ also reveals the love of God. You'll never understand how much God loves you until you see the Cross, because Jesus Christ was God in the flesh, dying on the cross for you and for me. Jesus died because He loved you. God so loved the world that He gave. The Scripture says that "God commendeth His love toward us, in that, while we were yet sinners, Christ died for us." He could have called 72,000 angels to come to His rescue, the Scripture says, and the human race would have been separated from God forever; but God loved us so much that He sent His Son to die. Christ hung on that cross for you; He said, "It is finished," and voluntarily gave up His spirit in order that you and I might live.

And the cross of Christ declares that it is the only way of salvation. You cannot be saved by your good works, by philanthropic deeds, by any other way than through the cross of Jesus Christ. As you receive and trust Him, committing yourself to Him, you can be saved from hell and *made new* here and now.

Selected Bibliography

Boa, Kenneth. *Cults, World Religions, and You.* Wheaton, Illinois: Victor Books, 1977.

Breese, Dave. *The Marks of Cults.* Wheaton, Illinois: Victor Books, 1975.

Chang, Lit-sen. *Zen Existentialism.* Phillipsburg, New Jersey: Presbyterian and Reformed Publishing Company, 1969.

Gerstner, John. *The Theology of the Major Sects.* Grand Rapids: Baker Books, 1960.

Horowitz, Irving (ed.). *Science, Sin, and Scholarship.* Cambridge, Massachusetts: The MIT Press, 1980.

Means, Pat. *The Mystical Maze.* San Bernardino, California: Here's Life Publishers, 1976.

Petersen, William J. *Those Curious New Cults.* New Canaan, Connecticut: Keats Publishing, Inc., 1973.

Weldon, John and Levitt, Zola. *The Transcendental Explosion.* Portland, Oregon: Harvest House, 1977.